SCUBA SCHOOLS INTERNAT

D0499104

Open Water Diver

MANUAL
3RD EDITION

DISCLAIMER:

The information contained in the SSI training materials is intended to give an individual enrolled in a training course a broad perspective of the diving activity. There are many recommendations and suggestions regarding the use of standard and specialized equipment for the activity. Not all of the equipment discussed in the training material can, or will, be used in this activity. The choice of equipment and techniques used in the course is determined by the location of the activity, the environmental conditions and other factors.

A choice of equipment and techniques cannot be made until the dive site is surveyed immediately prior to the dive. Based on the dive site, the decision should be made regarding which equipment and techniques shall be used. The decision belongs to the dive leader and the individual enrolled in the training course.

The intent of all SSI training materials is to give individuals as much information as possible in order for individuals to make their own decisions regarding the diving activity, what equipment should be used and what specific techniques may be needed. The ultimate decision on when and how to dive is for the individual diver to make.

First Edition
    First Printing, 1/90
    Second Printing, 9/90
Second Edition
    First Printing, 11/91
Third Edition
    First Printing, 12/95
    Second Printing, 3/97
    Third Printing, 9/98
    Fourth Printing, 3/00
    Fifth Printing, 5/01

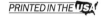
PRINTED IN THE USA

SCUBA SCHOOLS INTERNATIONAL
2619 Canton Court • Fort Collins, CO 80525-4498
(970) 482-0883 • Fax (970) 482-6157

Contents

Acknowledgments

EDITOR IN CHIEF	ROBERT A. CLARK
CONSULTANTS	ROBERT A. CLARK ED CHRISTINI DOUGLAS KELLY DENNIS PULLEY JOHN STEVES LEN TODISCO
STAFF WRITER	DON FREEMAN
PRODUCTION STAFF	DAVID M. PRATT, Art Director BETSY MUSSO, Graphic Artist
PHOTOGRAPHERS	GREG OCHOCKI BLAKE MILLER CHARLES ARNESON
CONTRIBUTING EDITORS	JEAN GREGOR BERT KOBAYASHI LAURIE HUMPAL
PROOFING EDITOR	LINDA CLARK
TECHNICAL EDITORS	JEAN GREGOR BERT KOBAYASHI BRUCE JAMESON PAUL CAPUTO DAVE MORGRIDGE TERRY NICKLIN MIKE WARD TAMOTSU ARAKAWA JAIMIE VIVES JAY SMITH JOHN WALL DEE WHITE BOB SCHAIBLE JACK GADBOIS JERE HALLENBECK DAVE FARRAR TOM BARTLEY JACK HOLMAN MARK LAYTON GEORGE BRANDT DAN ORR KIM WALKER BARBARA WILLINGHAM

Foreword

Welcome to the spectacular underwater world and your place in it. You are about to cross over into a new dimension of our Earth's many awesome and beautiful offerings, as well as a new dimension of your life's experiences. Scuba diving is the unique adventure which brings these two realms together.

Three-fourths of our colorful planet is under water, most of which has never been seen by human beings. These underwater regions can be enchanting, but because they are out of the human's natural element, the potential for hazard should be appreciated. Recreational scuba diving is easy, fun, and enjoyable, but it must be taken seriously. The skills needed to master diving are not difficult to learn, but must be learned well and practiced responsibly. Responsible divers must make efforts to keep proficient in the skills of diving.

This is why it is the privilege of only the *certified diver* to enter into this most ancient of new frontiers, and to join the growing, close-knit international community of divers who observe and explore, and even make their careers in the open waters of the world. Before you begin your course, there are a few important pieces of information you need to know.

CERTIFICATION

There are basically two types of diving: snorkeling and scuba diving. The *snorkeler* is skilled in the use of mask, fins, snorkel, and the buoyancy compensator, or "BC." The *scuba diver* has all the knowledge of the snorkeler but goes on to learn and become proficient in the operation of underwater breathing equipment, including air cylinder and breathing regulator, and gauges to monitor pressure, depth, time, and direction, which results in scuba certification. The word scuba stands for *Self-Contained Underwater Breathing Apparatus.*

Knowledge of scuba equipment and its proper use will greatly increase the possibility of the diver's enjoyment and comfort and greatly decrease the possibility that the diver will be hurt or will damage the diving environment. This is why certification is required by dive stores, resorts, air stations and charter boat operations before breathing equipment can be rented, cylinders filled, or diving services provided.

In order to obtain certification a diver must successfully complete a required course of instruction in both classroom and water settings. Most courses are designed to give students conceptual knowledge of the physics of diving, such as the effects of varying atmospheric pressures, the proper function of diving equipment, and the physiology of diving, such as

In order to obtain certification a diver must successfully complete a required course of instruction in both classroom and water settings.

how the human body must adjust for temperatures and depths, ascents and descents. They also cover safe diving practices and introduce and stress protection of the underwater environment.

When a student successfully completes classroom training, pool (or confined water) training, open water dives, and a final exam, a certification card is issued. This "C-card" and accompanying log book document that, at the end of the Open Water Diver course, the individual is proficient in basic skills of scuba diving. One can only remain a comfortable, proficient diver by diving. If you do not log enough open water dives to feel both comfortable and proficient, or you have not been diving for the last six months, then SSI recommends a Scuba Skills Update in order to be comfortable and to maintain proficiency as an open water diver.

STATEMENT OF RELATIONSHIP IN THE CERTIFICATION PROCESS

As a scuba diving student, it is important to understand the relationship of each participant in the diver certification process, and the responsibilities of each participant during the teaching process.

Scuba Schools International

Scuba Schools International (SSI) is a company whose primary function is to develop, produce and distribute educational programs and teaching materials for the training of recreational dive leaders and recreational scuba divers through a network of Authorized Dealers. The Open Water Diver course is the first in a series of programs used by the Authorized Dealer for the training and certification of recreational divers. SSI provides the products and programs used by the Authorized Dealer for the training and certification of recreational divers. SSI provides the Dealer and its staff with training in the use of the SSI educational programs and materials based on established training guidelines and standards. SSI provides these programs and materials and issues certification cards to SSI instructors through Authorized Dealers as a service.

SSI Authorized Dealer

Authorized Dealers of SSI products and programs are independently owned and operated dive businesses. These dive businesses, including retail dive stores, resorts, educational institutions and charter boats, are the cornerstone of the SSI Dealer system. The business owner's financial and personal commitment to the business is the best assurance of quality service to the consumer. Because of these commitments, the business is ideally positioned to ensure that the consumer receives the highest quality product. The business accomplishes this by monitoring the quality of its training programs and the adherence to standards by, and the performance of, its instructors. SSI's experience with this system since 1970 has proven to us that such dive businesses unquestionably provide the highest quality products and programs available to the consumer.

SSI Instructor

An active, certified SSI Instructor uses the SSI programs in the training of recreational divers and follows the procedures established by the SSI Authorized Dealer in accordance with the SSI Training Standards and guidelines. The Instructor's commitment is to ensure the integrity of the Open Water Diver program (or continuing education program) and to provide the student with sufficient time to develop the necessary scuba skills. This includes the Instructor making the students aware that the SSI programs are a progressive process. This means that during training the students become less dependent on the Instructor and more dependent on themselves, so that by the time they have completed the course of instruction they are prepared and confident to go diving without the supervision of an Instructor.

SSI Student

The SSI student may expect state-of-the-art training materials from SSI, quality programs and equipment from the SSI Authorized Dealer, and quality instruction (with the opportunity to learn at the student's own pace) from the SSI certified Instructor. The student should understand that, beginning with the Open Water Diver Course, the goal of the program is to make the student feel comfortable scuba diving without the Instructor. The student should also understand that SSI designs the systems, but does not do the actual instruction and cannot be physically present during classes. Therefore, SSI's ability to control anything beyond the system itself is extremely limited.

Should the student feel dissatisfied or uncomfortable with any phase of the scuba training program, the student may choose to inform one or all of the following: the SSI certified Instructor, the SSI Authorized Dealer, or SSI Headquarters.

LEARNING TO DIVE: THE SSI INTEGRATED SYSTEM

There are various approaches to diving instruction and more than one way to obtain certification. However, through years of experience in the field and observations of what works and what doesn't work in the training of divers, the staff at SSI (Scuba Schools International) has designed a multimedia, integrated instructional system which we believe to be the most efficient way to train competent open water divers in the shortest period of time.

The system relies on six basic elements: this text and accompanying study guide, video tapes, lectures and diving lessons given by instructors, and the diver's exhibited proficiency and confidence in the real world of open water diving.

This kind of system works because it reinforces learning through variety as well as repetition. The student reads a section of the textbook, then answers corresponding questions in the study guide. Next, a video of the same lesson is viewed, either at home or in the classroom. The instructor then reinforces the material for the third time through lecture and discussion sessions. Finally, newly learned skills are performed in the water

Newly learned skills are performed in the water under the supervision of the Instructor.

under the supervision of the Instructor. The sequence of these steps will vary based on the Instructor's style, and the time frame for the particular course.

The objective of SSI's *Open Water Diver* system is to teach the important basics of diving while avoiding bogging the student down with unnecessary material more appropriately reserved for advanced diving instruction.

Your SSI Open Water Diver Manual is divided into six main parts which parallel in a logical sequence the progression of what divers need to know.

Chapter 1 — Snorkeling covers the equipment necessary for snorkeling, and the skills and techniques needed for the proper selection, maintenance, and use of such equipment.

Chapter 2 — Scuba Diving goes beyond the basic equipment of the snorkeler to the more specialized equipment of the scuba diver, and covers techniques unique to scuba.

Chapter 3 — Adapting the Body to Water and Pressure takes the now fully-equipped diver under water. This important section deals with how the senses of hearing and sight, and the temperature of the body adjust to the unfamiliar underwater environment. It also covers how the respiratory system works, procedures the diver must follow in order to adjust the body for breathing under water, and precautions the diver must take to ensure safety and comfort.

Chapter 4 — Depth, Time, and the Diver explains the physics of pressure, how it affects the body at depth, and how the diver must compensate for pressure changes when descending, ascending, surfacing, and making repetitive dives.

Chapter 5 — The Aquatic Environment discusses various water environments, water movement and how it applies to the diver, and introduces some of the life forms the diver can expect to see under water.

Chapter 6 — Let's Go Diving!, the final section, is a review of the main points covered in the manual, and introduces divers to dive travel, the various diving environments and continuing education opportunities that are available.

Built into the system are specific criteria for the Instructor to present and on which to test the student. The requirements are so specific, in fact, that you must demonstrate proficiency in them all before becoming certified. However, the SSI program allows each student to be able to learn at his or her own pace. No one should be pushed through or left out. We want you to have fun diving and the only way to have fun is to first be competent.

You see, ability equals comfort, and comfort equals enjoyment. The SSI system works by teaching you the *abilities* you must have in order to be a scuba diver. When you become *comfortable and proficient* with your ability and knowledge, your Instructor will certify you as an open water scuba diver. It is our commitment to be with you every step of the way, from the time your interest is first sparked by colorful photographs and stories of exciting adventure from the underwater world, to the presentation of your own passport to this new realm—your certification card. It is then that you can truly enjoy the underwater realm.

CONTINUING EDUCATION: THE SSI LEVELS OF CERTIFICATION

Now, as a note to you before you begin your course, SSI would like you to know that the objective of our *Open Water Diver* program is not to make you an expert in the dynamics of water movement, or a professional biophysicist; we want to help you learn the basics of scuba diving. What you choose to do with this new knowledge is up to you.

However, once you begin diving you may want to learn more about this exciting sport. With SSI, there are many opportunities to increase your diving knowledge and experience, plus you can gain recognition along every step of the way.

SSI's Specialty Diver Program

SSI's Specialty Diver Program is a library of many topics you can choose from to meet your individual needs. Select the courses that are both interesting and fit your regional location. Choose from *Boat Diving, Deep Diving, Wreck Diving, Night/Limited Visibility Diving, Computer Diving* and a whole lot more.

SSI's Specialty Diver Program is a library of many topics you can choose from to meet your individual needs.

SSI's Total DiveLog flowchart

Take two Specialty Courses and log twelve dives and you qualify as a Specialty Diver. Take a total of four Specialty Courses and log twenty-four dives, and you qualify as an *Advanced Open Water Diver*. To earn the prestigious *Master Diver* rating you must log 50 dives, complete four Specialty Courses and the *Diver Stress and Rescue* course. SSI is unique in that we require training plus logged dives to earn advanced levels of certification such as *Specialty Diver, Advanced Open Water Diver* or *Master Diver*. It is the combination of knowledge and experience that truly makes you a comfortable and confident diver. SSI was the first agency to require logged dives plus training for advanced certification.

SSI's Total DiveLog flowchart, shown both here and in the front of your SSI DiveLog, explains the entire SSI levels of certification.

SSI's Platinum Diver Program

SSI was also the first agency to introduce the concept of diver recognition cards. These prestigious cards are earned simply by logging dives, no additional training is required. So don't forget to start your career off with a good habit of logging dives—they really do count! Our Platinum Diver Program set the standard for other recognition programs with our *Century Diver, Gold 500 Diver, Platinum 1000 Diver* and *Platinum Pro 5000 Diver* cards.

Our Platinum Diver Program set the standard for other recognition programs with our Century Diver, Gold 500 Diver, Platinum 1000 Diver and Platinum Pro 5000 Diver cards.

SSI's Scuba Skills Update Program

You should maintain proficient scuba skills by actively diving. If you've not been diving for a while, it is recommended that you take a Scuba Skills Update. A good rule of thumb is if you've not been diving within the last six months, you should take a Scuba Skills Update.

All right, now you're ready to begin that first step in your diving career—becoming a certified scuba diver! We do hope that you catch the spirit of diving, and that you recognize this sport for what it can be—a lifetime of fun and adventure.

Let's Get Started!

You're ready to begin that first step in your diving career—becoming a certified scuba diver!

Snorkeling

CHAPTER 1

Chapter 1: Snorkeling

INTRODUCTION

Diving developed in response to the intrigue water has always held for people. Recreational diving, however, is quite new. Through the 1950s and '60s, diving was limited to a few water-oriented people. What makes it accessible to the general public now is that today's equipment is designed to assist the diver, which makes diving comfortable and therefore enjoyable. Diving's foundation is equipment; that's why it is referred to as an *equipment-intensive* sport.

Each piece of equipment you will use was developed as the answer to a perceived need, and most of the risks inherent to diving can be minimized through the proper use of this equipment. Similarly, your needs as a novice diver are met by equipment, and risks are minimized by your familiarization and practice with the equipment.

In addition to being a necessary element of diving, the right kind of equipment can be the difference between an enjoyable dive and one plagued by problems and frustrations. Proper equipment enables a diver not only to see, swim, and breathe in the water, but also provides a degree of comfort and confidence which can actually transform an otherwise alien world into a friendly and familiar place. Your Instructor and local SSI Authorized Dealer are your best consultants for selecting and purchasing equipment. They are there to help you with your training and equipment needs, so feel free to utilize this valuable resource (Figure 1-1).

Figure 1-1 Your Instructor and local SSI Authorized Dealer are your best consultants for selecting and purchasing equipment.

Let's start by looking at the basic equipment which we have termed snorkeling equipment. While this equipment can be used by snorkelers, it is also the basic equipment required by all scuba divers and it provides a comfortable introduction to your new underwater environment.

SNORKELING EQUIPMENT

The most apparent obstacles for early divers were the inability to see clearly and breathe under water, and the human's very limited mobility in water. The four basic pieces of the snorkeler's equipment begin to overcome these obstacles. The mask, fins, snorkel, and buoyancy compensator empower the diver by approximating the natural dry-land abilities to see, breathe, and move about. Protective divewear and the weight belt also contribute to the diver's comfort and ability. When purchasing snorkeling equipment you should consider that some snorkeling equipment may not be adequate for scuba diving.

The four basic pieces of the snorkeler's equipment.

THE MASK

The human eye is not designed to work well when immersed in water. Vision is blurry and the field of vision limited. Since the eye is designed to see through air, which is of light density, rather than water, with its much heavier density, what is needed is to simulate the eye's natural medium by surrounding it with a pocket of air.

The first attempts at this produced something akin to the modern swimming goggle; but this design had shortcomings for divers because pressure at depth tightened them against the face, causing discomfort and the risk of injury to the eyes and surrounding tissues.

A larger, more flexible enclosure was necessary. This was accomplished by the single lens mask which surrounds not only the eyes, but also the nose, making it possible to exhale into the mask and bring the pressure inside into balance with external pressure (Figure 1-2). The design works and therefore has changed very little since its invention.

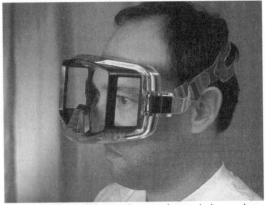

Figure 1-2   The single lens mask surrounds not only the eyes, but also the nose, making it possible to exhale into the mask and bring the pressure inside into balance with external pressure.

Choosing a Mask

The mask is your window to the underwater world and probably the most important piece of equipment you will ever purchase for diving. There are two basic types of masks: the *low volume* and the *high volume* (Figure 1-3). The one you choose depends mostly on personal preference.

Figure 1-3   There are two basic types of masks: the low volume and the high volume.

The low volume mask has a small air space and a pocket for the nose. It is a favorite of snorkelers and scuba divers because it is an easy mask from which to eliminate, or "clear," water that has gotten inside.

Some high volume masks may also increase the field of vision by using transparent side plates. This mask has a larger internal volume.

Clear or colored silicone is the most common material used for mask skirts and straps. Black rubber has been used in the past, but clear silicone is more versatile because it lets in more light, eliminates the tunnel vision caused by a non-transparent mask, and requires little maintenance. Any equipment made of silicone, however, can be discolored by the sun.

Some masks offer a one-way purge valve which allows water inside to escape when the diver exhales into the mask through the nose (Figure 1-4). It makes mask clearing easier and, some find, more convenient; however, you will learn how to comfortably clear any mask.

Figure 1-4   Some masks offer a one-way purge valve which allows water inside to escape when the diver exhales into the mask through the nose.

Corrective Lenses

The diver whose vision needs correction has several options. The nearsighted diver may choose to correct vision with optical lenses measured in *diopters*—corrective lenses offered by manufacturers to replace stock lenses in their particular mask models (Figure 1-5). Vision can also be corrected exactly by integrat-

Figure 1-5   The nearsighted diver may choose to correct vision with optical lenses measured in diopters.

ing prescription lenses into dive masks. In this case prescription lenses are ground and then affixed directly to the inside of the mask lenses by a qualified optical lab. It is also possible to use contact lenses. All vision correction considerations and decisions should be made only with the consent and approval of your eye doctor and coordinated through your eye doctor and dive retailer.

Mask Features (Figure 1-6)

There are several important features to look for when choosing a mask:

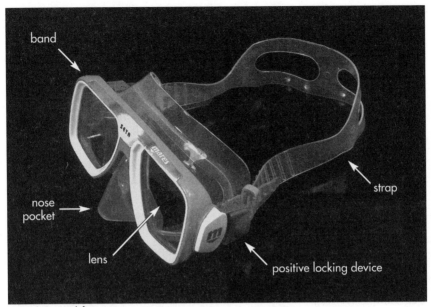

Figure 1-6 Mask features.

- **Lens.** The lens should be made of tempered glass. Mask lenses come from the factory with a film on them which needs to be cleaned off with non-abrasive, liquid detergent and warm water before using an anti-fogging solution.

- **Band.** The lens retainer should be noncorrosive—hard plastic or stainless steel.

- **Strap.** The strap should adjust easily and lock in place. It should also be split at the back of the head or wide enough to adhere to the head securely; a narrow single band slips up and down too easily. For added comfort, you may want to replace your strap with a neoprene mask strap. Many divers consider them to be more comfortable and easier to use (Figure 1-7).

Figure 1-7 For added comfort, you may want to replace your strap with a neoprene mask strap.

- **Positive Locking Device.** Your mask should come equipped with a positive locking device which allows you to quickly adjust the mask strap and then lock it in place.

- **Nose Pockets.** Nose or finger pockets built into masks are used for equalizing pressure inside the ears and sinuses as the diver descends and pressure increases. Equalization is discussed in detail in Chapter 3.

Fitting the Mask

Masks differ, as do facial contours. The objective in finding a mask that fits is to match the mask skirt and your face. The soft material of the skirt has to fit comfortably without pinching or applying more pressure in one place than another; there should be no pressure points where the mask is uncomfortable against your face. The skirt should form a seal with your face. Quality masks use a double seal which is more comfortable and further reinforces sealing ability.

To check a mask for fit, tilt your head back and lay the mask on your face without using the strap (Figure 1-8a). The force of gravity alone should keep a good fitting mask in place. Run a finger around the mask skirt to make sure the entire sealing edge touches your face and that no hair (including facial hair) is between the mask seal and your face. Then inhale gently through your nose to hold the mask against the face, tilt your head forward and look straight ahead. The mask should stay on with only a gentle inhalation and you should not detect any air leak (Figure 1-8b). Use this test with several different models to find the one which fits best and is most comfortable.

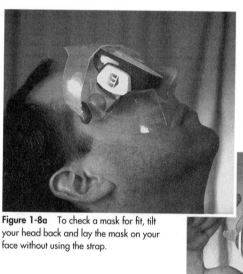

Figure 1-8a   To check a mask for fit, tilt your head back and lay the mask on your face without using the strap.

Figure 1-8b   The mask should stay on with only a gentle inhalation and you should not detect any air leak.

FINS AND FOOTWEAR

Once you can see under water, the next step is learning how to propel yourself under water. Conventional swimming is limited by both range of movement and the length of time it can be prolonged, given normal strength and endurance. Fins substantially increase the power and utility of the bare foot, and also greatly reduce the energy needed to move the body forward. They enable swimmers to move over greater distances for longer periods of time without tiring.

Choosing Fins

Fins come in two basic styles: the *full-foot* and the *open-heel*. Full-foot fins fit like shoes and come in standard sizes. Open-heel fins come in small, medium, large, and extra-large sizes and hold the foot in place with an adjustable heel strap. The open-heel fin and wet suit boot should be considered one unit and should be selected and fitted with one another.

Fin Features

Materials, designs, and features vary among fins, and just as with the mask you need to know these variations when choosing fins for your particular needs:

■ **Materials.** Fin blade materials include black rubber, polyurethane, thermoplastic, and various plastic composites (Figure 1-9). The type of materials used by the manufacturers will vary based on the design, performance and use of the fin. Many manufacturers use a combination of materials in order to accomplish multiple ben-

Figure 1-9   Fin blade materials include black rubber, polyurethane, thermoplastic, and various plastic composites.

efits. The fin that is best suited for you will depend on your physical size, leg strength, environmental conditions and, most of all, comfort and fit. Your SSI Dealer or Instructor can assist you in finding the best possible fin for you.

■ **Buoyancy.** Some fins sink and some float. A fin that sinks can be easily lost in deep water, but might be easier to find in shallow water if it sinks to the bottom. A fin that floats poses two problems: If it floats to the surface it can also float away, and its constant tendency to float will uncomfortably lift the diver's legs while swimming. A fin as close as possible to neutrally buoyant (neither sinks nor floats) is a good compromise, staying close at hand if it accidentally comes off.

■ **Fit.** An open-heel fin with adjustable strap can compensate for slight variations in the size of the foot and wet suit boot because of expansion and contraction, and can also permit the use of various thicknesses of boots (Figure 1-10). The open-heel and wet suit boot should be fitted together and be selected at the same time. Using a fin that fits well can prevent physical problems such as chafing and cramps, and can also keep the fin from falling off. Though full-foot fins can be well fitted, they are not worn over wet suit boots so they are limited to use in comfortable temperatures.

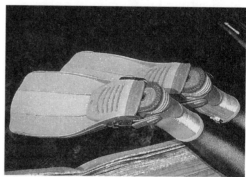

Figure 1-10   Open-heel fin with adjustable strap.

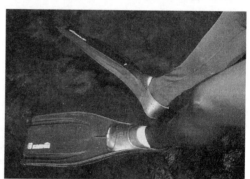

Figure 1-11   The full-foot fin.

For extra comfort, the full-foot fin can be worn with a special sock of lycra or neoprene (Figure 1-11).

■ **Vented and Non-vented Fins.** Vented and non-vented fins are made of materials much like those used in regular fins. Manufacturers design that aspect of the fin to accomplish a specific performance in the water. The use of vented or non-vented fins will be based on the type of diving you'll be doing, as well as comfort and fit. Your SSI Dealer or Instructor can assist you in making the right choice for you.

■ **Length and Flexibility.** Choosing a particular blade strength and length is a personal decision. Larger, stiffer blades may provide more speed but may be harder to propel, and would therefore be inappropriate for a diver who doesn't have the leg strength to use them for extended periods. Your SSI Dealer will help you find fins well suited to your experience level and physical capability.

Fitting the Fins

With open-heel fins, adjust the strap to keep the booted foot firmly in place. Then try to kick the fin off. It should stay on, and the foot pocket should neither bind, pinch, nor allow the foot too much excess movement. Also, the toes should not jam, and overall fit should not be so tight that it restricts circulation.

Though the full-foot fin is not adjustable and is not worn with a boot, the same rules of fit and comfort apply. To test the fit, stand and attempt to lift your heel out; it should stay snugly in place.

Like choosing a mask, finding the fins that are right for you is a personal decision. Whatever else you decide on, it is of primary importance that the fins fit well, are comfortable, and are suited to your size and strength.

THE SNORKEL

After vision and movement, the next fundamental skill for the diver is breathing while exploring in water. The snorkel allows relaxed exploration at the surface, solving the problem of having to constantly raise the head above water to breathe while swimming.

The snorkel allows relaxed exploration at the surface.

Choosing a Snorkel

There are a few options available when choosing a snorkel, but for the most part a workable design has been agreed upon. The two main considerations are breathing comfort and fit.

Snorkel Features

There are several features you may want to look for when selecting a snorkel. While these features may not affect the function of the snorkel, they will increase breathing comfort and fit:

■ *Bore Style and Size.* A snorkel will either have a solid or flexible bore. The flexible snorkel is designed so that the snorkel hangs out of the way of the regulator. Solid bore snorkels should be contoured for proper positioning of the mouthpiece and reduced drag in the water.

Most manufacturers recommend a larger bore size for easier breathing (Figure 1-12).

■ *Self-Draining Purge Valve.* Some snorkels are equipped with a self-draining purge valve below the mouthpiece (Figure 1-13). Excess water is collected in a reservoir and automatically cleared from the snorkel with each exhalation, keeping the mouthpiece free of water.

■ *Mouthpiece.* Your snorkel should have a soft, comfortable mouthpiece that fits your mouth. The mouthpiece may also swivel so you can adjust it to the most comfortable position. Some snorkels are designed so the mouthpiece can be replaced.

■ *Dry or Semi-dry Vent.* Another added feature is a dry or semi-dry vent on top of the snorkel. Most manufacturers offer their own patented design. The dry or semi-dry vent helps prevent water on the surface from splashing into the snorkel bore and entering the mouthpiece, helping to keep water out and reducing the amount of water in the tube (Figure 1-14).

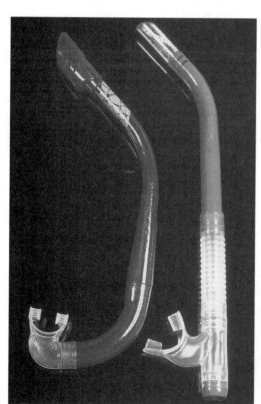

Figure 1-13   Some snorkels are equipped with a self-draining purge valve below the mouthpiece.

Figure 1-14   The dry or semi-dry vent helps prevent water on the surface from splashing into the snorkel bore and entering the mouthpiece.

Figure 1-12   A snorkel will either have a solid or flexible bore.

PROTECTIVE DIVEWEAR: EXPOSURE SUITS

Water absorbs body heat twenty-five times faster than air, so even warm water will "pull" heat from the body (Figure 1-15). Ideally, the normal body temperature of 98.6°F (37°C) should be maintained in water. This requires varying layers of protective wear depending on the duration of the dive, the temperature of the water and the particular needs of the diver.

Tolerance to cold can vary greatly from one person to another, and between two divers of similar physique, one can get cold while the other remains comfortable. Accordingly, exposure suit needs are not exactly predictable. There are general suggestions about the type of exposure suit you're likely to need based on temperature ranges. However, the amount of protection you use will depend ultimately on preference, except in colder waters where a dry suit is definitely necessary.

We will first look at warm water dive skins, the favorite for snorkelers and warm water divers, and then go on to wet suits and dry suits which gradually increase in thermal protection.

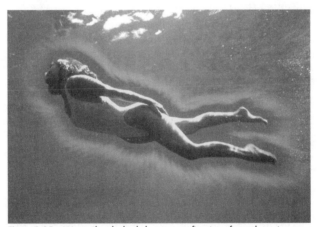

Figure 1-15 Water absorbs body heat twenty-five times faster than air, so even warm water will "pull" heat from the body.

Warm Water Dive Skins

At temperatures above 91°F (33°C) most divers will stay comfortable without protective wear. But even in the rare case of diving in water this warm it is a good idea at least to be protected from sunburn, the marine environment, and equipment that might cause chafing.

Dive skins are made from a variety of materials, some of which include lycra/nylon or polypropylene. There are also bonded fabrics available, such as Darlexx®, Polartec® and others which are actually laminates of various fabrics which, when combined, create a warmer, better suit. Laminated fabrics may be warmer, more waterproof, more wind-proof, more breathable, and more neutrally buoyant than other material.

Dive skins become more popular each year as technology improves the quality of the fabrics available (Figure 1-16). Plus, many of these laminated fabrics are as warm as a 2mm wet suit, without the added bulk or buoyancy of neoprene. Plus, the stretchy, comfortable fabrics tend to fit more people than off-the-rack wet suits. Another popular use for the dive skin is wearing it as an undergarment to aid in getting in and out of the wet suit, which can be pulled on and off arms, legs, and shoulders much easier over the smooth fabric. If a dive skin is used under a wet suit, the two should be *fitted* together.

Figure 1-16 Dive skins become more popular each year as technology improves the quality of the fabrics available.

Your SSI Dealer can advise you of any improvements to warm water dive skins, or to any new fabrics and styles that are currently available.

Wet Suit

Wet suits are made of foam neoprene. Your body will still get wet while wearing a "wet" suit, but your body *heat* will pass through this extra layer of insulation much slower, keeping you warm longer. They are available as one-piece jumpsuits, or as separate components in various styles and configurations.

Choosing a Wet Suit

The decisions you make regarding wet suits will involve variations in thickness and coverage. Thicknesses vary between two and seven millimeters. Coverage ranges from the limited protection of the *wet suit vest* which only covers the torso and the *shorty* with its short arms and legs, to a full-coverage wet suit which can be made up of pants and jacket, *Farmer Johns* and jacket, or a one-piece jump suit (Figure 1-17).

Most recreational diving is done in water temperatures between about 50°F to 80°F (10°C to 27°C). Coverage and thickness preferences come into play at the warm and cold extremes of this range, but it is generally agreed that full wet suits should be worn from 65° to 75°F (18° to 24°C), and that a hood is required below 65°F (18°C). Gloves offer excellent protection against cold and abrasion, however, many dive resorts no longer allow divers to use gloves when diving on coral reefs.

At extremely cold temperatures you can use a combination of wet suit components. Layering garments works as well under water as it does on land. A shorty or a jacket can be worn over a Farmer John, for instance. Movement becomes restricted, however, as you combine pieces or use thicker material.

Wet Suit Features

Some suits will feature zippers at the wrists, ankles, waist, or up the sides. These make dressing easier but also allow more water to seep into the suit.

Other accessories added for convenience and comfort include

Shorty.   Farmer   One-Piece Jump
            John.   Suit.

Figure 1-17

pockets, knee and elbow pads, and spine pads which conform to the diver's back and provide protection between the diver's back and the scuba tank, as well as lessen the exchange of warmed water inside the suit with cold outside water, which causes more body heat loss. Some suits feature attached hoods which help prevent the leakage of water down the spine. Some wet suits have additional wrist and neck seals and can be termed "semi-dry" due to the way these seals effectively reduce the transfer of water in and out of the suit.

Wet Suit Fit

A good fit is one of the most important considerations when choosing a wet suit. If the suit is too loose it will allow water to circulate inside it, cooling the body. If it is too tight it can restrict circulation and movement, cause pressure spots, and make a diver exert excess energy while fighting against its tight fit.

The suit should be snug without binding or pinching, and it should not have gaps or sags under the arms or at the crotch. The neck, wrist, waist, and ankle openings should be tight enough to prevent water from sloshing in, but loose enough to allow comfort and free blood circulation.

A custom-fitted suit is ideal and costs only slightly more than an off-the-rack suit. Having a suit which conforms to your body cuts down on sags and gaps, ensuring less water exchange and therefore less heat loss and greater comfort. The thicker the wet suit material, the more important fit becomes.

Dry suit

The dry suit provides complete protection against cold water (Figure 1-18). Unlike the wet suit, it keeps the body relatively dry. Dry suits can be made of neoprene, rubber, or laminated synthetic materials. An inflator hose is attached to the suit so it can be inflated to compensate for compression as the diver descends and pressure increases. This prevents an uncomfortable *suit squeeze* and maintains the same degree of thermal protection regardless of depth.

You may want to consider using a dry suit in waters below 60° F (16° C). Some divers prefer them at higher temperatures. This type of suit is used mainly in areas where the water is consistently colder.

Figure 1-18   The dry suit provides complete protection against cold water.

It is not recommended that you dive in a dry suit unless you have had either an orientation to dry suits or a complete SSI Dry Suit Specialty Course. The Dry Suit Specialty is available from your SSI Authorized Dealer.

WEIGHT BELT

Exposure suits provide protection against cold and injury. However, in solving one problem, they

> **It is not recommended that you dive in a dry suit unless you have had either an orientation to dry suits or a complete SSI Dry Suit Specialty Course.**

create another. Most exposure suits "float," making the diver's body *positively buoyant.* The weight belt counteracts that added buoyancy and also helps the diver whose body is naturally buoyant, regardless of added buoyancy, to get below the surface (Figure 1-19). This is especially necessary in salt water which further "buoys up" the body. Your objective in using a weight belt is to establish *neutral buoyancy*, a condition of neither floating nor sinking, but rather of being suspended weightless. Buoyancy will be discussed in detail in Chapter 3.

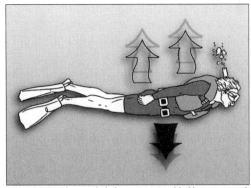

Figure 1-19   The weight belt counteracts added buoyancy and helps the diver get below the surface.

Choosing a Weight Belt

Some determinations regarding the weight belt can be made on land, but the most important determination—exactly how much weight the belt needs relative to your body and equipment—can be made only in the water. Your SSI Instructor can show you how to select the proper amount of weight for your belt. Other choices when selecting a weight belt include the material in the belt and various weight designs.

Weight Belt Features

■ *Belts.* The most common material used for the belt is webbed nylon. It is durable and can support plenty of weight. A variation on the nylon belt is one which includes a flexible depth compensating device which shrinks as the exposure suit compresses. A design which combines practicality and comfort is the

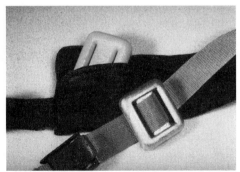

Pocket weight belt.   Webbed nylon weight belt.

pocket weight belt, which is made from both neoprene and nylon mesh. This design uses internal weight pockets to eliminate the bulk and discomfort of exposed weights. With weight pockets, weights also can be added or subtracted easily while the belt is being worn.

■ *Buckles.* The buckle of the belt should be made of a non-corrosive material and should be able to be opened with one hand for quick release.

■ *Weights.* Lead weights come in a variety of sizes, shapes, and weight values (Figure 1-20). Some lead weights feature vinyl coatings, available in colors, which protect boat and pool decks from scratches.

Another design is the soft weight, consisting of a sealed pouch full of lead shot. These pouches are available in various weight sizes and are used

Figure 1-20   Weights come in a variety of sizes, shapes, and weight values.

with pocket weight belts. Some consider shot-filled weights to be more comfortable because they can conform to the body, and more environmentally friendly should the weights be dropped or come loose while diving.

Integrated weight systems, which are available in some buoyancy compensators will be discussed in Chapter 2, Scuba Diving.

BUOYANCY COMPENSATOR: THE SNORKELING VEST

The ability to see, breathe, and move are necessary elements of snorkeling, but to enhance the efficiency and comfort of these elements, the diver's buoyancy needs to be controlled by a buoyancy compensator, or BC. The small *snorkeling vest* which fits like a bib provides the snorkeler "lift" at the surface (Figure 1-21). The inflated vest minimizes water resistance for swimming, keeps the lungs slightly higher so that water pressure is lessened and breathing is easier, and also helps keep the snorkel higher above the water surface. The diver adds or subtracts air as needed using an inflation tube or hose. Some models feature a CO_2 cartridge and detonator

Figure 1-21   The small snorkeling vest which fits like a bib provides the snorkeler "lift" at the surface.

which immediately inflates the vest if necessary. Snorkeling vests are also equipped with deflation mechanisms. Air is either allowed to escape slowly through the inflator hose, or in some models can be let out all at once through a *dump valve.*

Snorkeling vests should not be used for scuba diving. However, scuba diving BCs can be used for snorkeling. It is your decision whether to purchase a separate snorkeling vest for your future snorkeling experiences, however some type of flotation device is highly recommended.

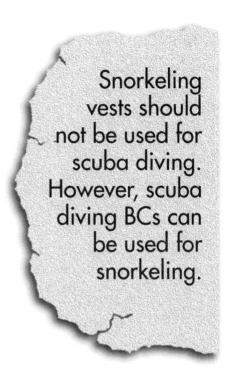

Snorkeling vests should not be used for scuba diving. However, scuba diving BCs can be used for snorkeling.

USING YOUR SNORKELING EQUIPMENT

Now that you've been introduced to the individual components, we'll look at the fundamental snorkeling ensemble—the mask, snorkel, fins, weight belt, and vest—in the setting where you'll be experiencing them in action, the water.

Most of the skills will be transferable from snorkeling to scuba; so, after covering basics, we'll go on to Chapter 2 in which some of the information will be repeated, but will be expanded on for use with scuba.

DRESSING

Putting on the Exposure Suit

The exposure suit needs to be put on in the proper order at the proper time. Follow the following steps in the right order (Figure 1-22, next page). A general rule for dressing is to do it right before the dive. If you put on your wet suit well before your entry you can become overheated.

1. **Pants.** From the hips down, fold the pants inside-out down to the knees (Figure 1-22a). Slip the legs in up to your knees, then roll the pants up over your thighs and hips, making sure the crotch fits snugly (Figure 1-22b).

2. **Boots.** For zipperless boots, roll the top of the boot down past the heel. Work the foot in as far as it will comfortably go, then roll the boot back up over the ankle. The boots can be tucked under the wet suit pants, or over the pants based on the type of diving environment. If your boots have zippers, rolling is not necessary (Figure 1-22c).

3. **Hood.** Holding the hood at the back, pull it from the forehead back over the top of the head so that your hair is completely covered. The skirt of the hood should be tucked neatly under the collar of the jacket. It may be easier to put the hood on first, then zip the jacket over it (Figure 1-22d).

4. **Jacket.** Put the wet suit jacket on one arm at a time (Figure 1-22e). Fit the sleeve openings around the wrists, then pull the sleeves all the way up to the underarms until they fit snugly without gaps or sags.

5. **Gloves.** The gloves are put on just like ordinary ones, but must be pulled snugly onto the fingers and wrists. Many divers prefer to wait and put on the gloves later so the fingers are free for other equipment donning and adjustment. You may wish to leave only one hand ungloved, then put the other on after all adjustments are made. Overlap the sleeves of your wet suit with the gloves to cut down on water seepage.

6. **Weight belt.** When all the pieces of the suit are in place, put on the weight belt (Figure 1-22f).

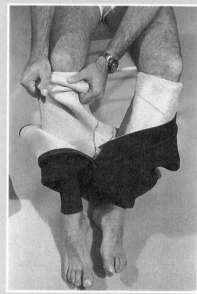

A. Fold the pants inside-out down to the knees...

D. The skirt of the hood should be tucked neatly under the collar of the jacket.

Figure 1-22   Putting on the exposure suit.

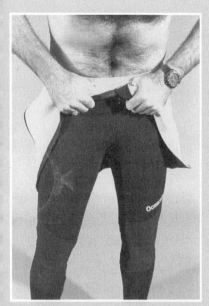

B. ... then roll the pants up over your thighs and hips.

C. The boots can be tucked under or over the pants.

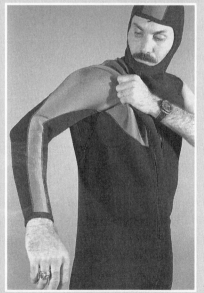

E. Put the wet suit jacket on one arm at a time.

F. Put on the weight belt.

WEIGHTING

Part 1: The Weight Belt

The weight belt should be adjusted to fit snugly, with the weights distributed evenly and positioned near the front of the hips (Figure 1-23). The buckle is positioned to open opposite of the BC strap buckle. In other words, adjust the buckles so that they open from opposite sides— the weight belt with right hand release and the BC with left hand release, or vice versa. The reason for this is that the two should never be confused. Weight belt ditching is a very important skill (covered in depth in Chapter 3), and you and your buddy need to know how to remove your own as well as each other's belt quickly and in the same way every

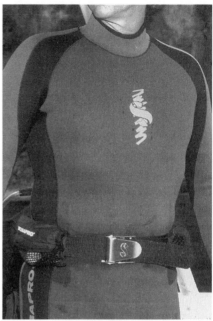

Figure 1-23   The weights distributed evenly and positioned near the front of the hips.

time. Also, the belt itself should be fitted so that there is approximately 2-4" of excess material when the belt is buckled. You may need to cut webbed nylon to length. Ask your SSI Dealer or Instructor to custom fit your weight belt for you.

Part 2: Proper Weighting

To fit your belt with the proper amount of weight, first get in the water while wearing all the other equipment. Move to a place where you can float, then with your vest deflated, add enough weight to make yourself neutrally buoyant: You'll neither sink nor float, and your eyes will rise to about water level when you inhale, and sink slightly below the surface when you exhale.

PUTTING ON THE EQUIPMENT

Buoyancy Compensator

The buoyancy compensator is easily donned when not yet combined with the tank for scuba use. Just put it on and make sure it fits your body correctly, that it is snug and that the straps are adjusted correctly. If it is too loose it can ride up when you're swimming on the surface or entering the water. It must not interfere with the removal or ditching of the weight belt.

Mask

When putting on the mask, place it on your face and then pull the strap over the back of your head (Figure 1-24a & b). The strap needs to be adjusted so that the mask is kept firmly and comfortably in place without over-tightening. When you have the strap where you want it, secure it.

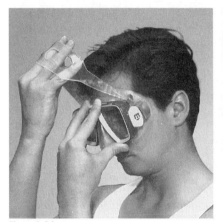

Figure 1-24a
Place the mask on your face...

Figure 1-24b
...then pull the strap over the back of your head.

Adjust a split strap, if so equipped, so that it holds to the upper and lower parts of the curvature at the back of your head, or as closely to this ideal position as possible. If the strap is too low or too high on your head the mask will leak (Figure 1-25).

Snorkel

The snorkel is positioned on the left side of the head and is attached to the mask strap by a *snorkel keeper*

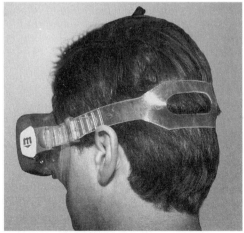

Figure 1-25   Ideal split strap position.

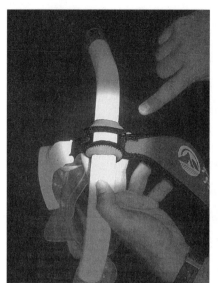

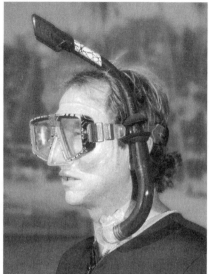

Figure 1-26 The snorkel is attached to the mask strap by a snorkel keeper.

Figure 1-27 The snorkel should be positioned so that the tube is straight up when the diver is looking down.

(Figure 1-26). There are many varieties of snorkel keepers on the market, but all perform the same function. You can adjust the position by moving the snorkel keeper up and down the snorkel bore, and by moving the keeper back and forth on the mask strap. The snorkel should be positioned so that the mouthpiece is comfortable in the mouth, and the tube is straight up when the diver is looking down into the water (Figure 1-27).

Fins

The fins can be put on either from a sitting position or by standing and using a buddy for support. If you do put them on while standing, secure yourself with one arm, then cross one leg over the other forming a figure "4" and pull on the fin (Figure 1-28). Because you become slightly less coordinated when wearing the fins on dry land, they are generally the last thing you put on, and only when near your point of entry. Under some conditions the fins can be donned after you enter the water.

Figure 1-28 If you put your fins on while standing, secure yourself with one arm, then cross one leg over the other forming a figure "4."

ENTERING THE WATER

You should always use the best entry possible for the given circumstances. The *best* entry is the **easiest, safest, and least disorienting** one. The entry should not jar or displace the equipment; and once you are in the water you should be able to see, breathe, and float.

> The *best* entry is the easiest, safest, and least disorienting one.

Before entering it is important to make a dive plan. Dive planning is covered in detail in subsequent chapters, but here are a few important points to consider: Which direction will you go and where will you exit? Be aware of currents and which way they will carry you. Next, survey your dive entry site to make sure there are no obstructions. Also, a buddy check should be done to make sure your equipment, as well as your buddy's, is assembled, adjusted, and operating correctly. At this time inflate your BCs so that you will float after your entry. Next, determine who will enter the water first.

The *controlled seated* entry is the easiest and least disorienting method. It is done from low pool decks, docks, or boat platforms, and only in calm water (Figure 1-29, page 24). While sitting on the edge with your legs dangling in the water, place both hands on one side of your body—holding on to the platform if possible. Then, support your body with your arms, turn and slip gently into the water. The advantages of this entry are that you maintain stability by having constant contact with the platform, and that there is very little impact with the water.

The *step-in*, or "giant stride," is the most common entry (Figure 1-30, page 24). It is done from a standing position on docks or boat dive-decks. The surface needs to be fairly firm so that balance can be maintained. Position yourself with fins together at the edge of the entry point, hold the mask in place with one hand and the weight belt with the other, then step out with one leg in front of the other—toes up, heels down—and enter the water with legs open "scissors" style. Hold your equipment in place until you surface and can see, breathe, and float.

A more appropriate entry from higher platforms is the *jumping entry*. When you leave the entry platform, bring the fins together, and keep them positioned horizontally so that you pierce the water and smoothly submerge (Figure 1-31, page 24). The fins will slow your entry into the water considerably, but it will still be necessary to secure your mask and weight belt as you jump.

Front roll entries are discouraged because they tend to leave the diver disoriented under water. In fact, the head-first aspect of any roll entry

Figure 1-29   The controlled seated entry.

Figure 1-30   The step-in, or "giant stride" entry.

Figure 1-31   The jumping entry.

Figure 1-32   The back roll entry.

makes the diver more vulnerable to disorientation and possible collision with an obstruction than a feet-first entry does. Sometimes you may need to do a *back roll* entry when boat diving (Figure 1-32). Though it has commonly been used, it can pose problems. In addition, any time a diver is near enough to the water's surface to consider a roll entry, a seated entry will probably suffice. It is recommended that you do a back roll entry only when there are no other options.

When making an entry from a shore or beach, again, use the easiest and safest method possible. If you enter on a beach with surf breaking near the shore, shuffle backwards with your fins on until deep enough to swim, then turn and swim out under or through the surf (Figure 1-33). If conditions are calm on shore, wade in without fins until about knee or waist-deep, put them on there, then swim out. (Beach entries and exits will be covered in depth in Chapter 5.)

Figure 1-33   If you enter on a beach with surf breaking near the shore, shuffle backwards with your fins on until deep enough to swim.

When using any method other than the seated entry, grip your mask and weight belt firmly to keep them in place during the entry, have the snorkel in your mouth, and the BC inflated (Figure 1-34). Enter the water one at a time, making sure that the area of your entry is clear. After surfacing, clear the area before your buddy enters, then give the OK sign. Watch your buddy enter, being ready to assist if necessary. In fact, as a general rule always be aware of your buddy's condition and whereabouts.

Figure 1-34   Grip your mask and weight belt firmly to keep them in place during the entry.

USING THE MASK

Once under water you will rely on some basic skills which will help you keep your vision clear and the mask in place and comfortable.

Warm air inside the lens condenses when cool water surrounds the mask. This causes the lens to fog and restrict vision. Eliminate this problem by coating the inside of the lens with *anti-fogging* solution before getting the mask wet (Figure 1-35). However, if you are using a new mask, you must first clean off a silicone film which coats the inside of the lens before using anti-fog. Do this with a mild, non-abrasive, liquid detergent and warm water. If the lens fogs while under water despite precautions, let a little water in and clear it.

Figure 1-35   Coat the inside of the lens with *anti-fogging* solution before getting the mask wet.

By now you've encountered the term *clearing the mask* a few times. In snorkeling, this is a simple procedure. Small amounts of water will inevitably get into the mask. To clear your mask come to the surface, or stand up if necessary, and lift the bottom of the mask with your thumbs, letting the water run out (Figure 1-36).

Figure 1-36   To clear your mask, come to the surface and lift the bottom of the mask with your thumbs, letting the water run out.

USING THE SNORKEL

The immediate benefit of breathing through a snorkel is your ability to float face down on the surface, resting and moving comfortably, without having to lift your head to breathe. Breathing with a snorkel is different from normal breathing. It is done in a three step process that helps ensure that you will always be able to breathe without interference from water in the tube. First, clear the snorkel by blowing a quick, sharp blast of air through it. This is called the *popping method* (Figure 1-37). You may need to clear again to remove any remaining water before breathing. Next, breathe cautiously through the snorkel. Lastly, hold that breath so that you have another "blast" saved for clearing. Get into the habit of this pattern: **Clear**, **Breathe**, and **Hold**, then repeat.

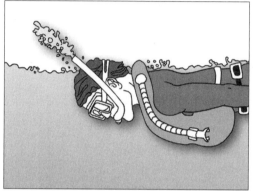

Figure 1-37   The popping method.

Water will enter the snorkel when you dive under water. The way to clear the snorkel while under water and ascending to the surface is called the *expansion method* (Figure 1-38). As you approach the surface, tilt your head back so that the snorkel tube is pointing downward, and then blow a small puff of air into it. This air expands due to lessening pressure as you rise toward the surface, and any remaining water is forced out.

Figure 1-38   The expansion method.

Snorkels equipped with self-draining purge valves are cleared mostly by the force of gravity with each exhalation, but expansion may work with this kind of snorkel. Any remaining water should be cleared by popping, just as with any other type of snorkel.

USING THE FINS

There are a few general rules about fin use you need to know before getting into the water. First, sometimes you'll need to walk with your fins on. It is awkward and almost impossible to walk forward with fins, let alone to walk at all. It is easier and safer to *shuffle* backwards on pool and boat decks, on the shore, and while entering and leaving shallow water.

Do not climb pool and boat ladders with fins on unless the ladder is designed for this use. Remove your fins and either hand them up, or loop your arms through the fin straps and carry them up (Figure 1-39). Be sure the BC is inflated in case you fall back into the water, and do not remove fins until you are near your point of exit; with other equipment on, it is very difficult to swim without them.

Figure 1-39   Remove your fins and either hand them up or loop your arms through the fin straps and carry them up.

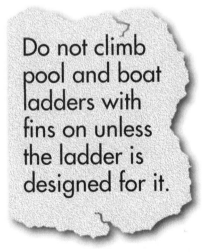

Do not climb pool and boat ladders with fins on unless the ladder is designed for it.

Fin Kicks

In the water the fins become an extension of your body, and turn your feet and legs into a powerful imitation of the sweeping tail of the dolphin. Fins allow the diver to move through the water smoothly and with much less effort than without them. The power gained by using fins while swimming, in fact, all but eliminates the need to use the hands or arms, which can be left relaxed at the sides, clasped in front of the body or carrying extra equipment. A comfortable diver will not use the hands or arms for swimming, except for negotiating turns.

Several different kicks are used in different situations. The *flutter kick* is the most basic and most often used (Figure 1-40). The legs are kept elongated and the toes pointed. The knees bend slightly and the relaxed ankles swing back and forth with the natural motion of the fins. The stroke is slow and powerful, utilizing the full length of the legs; it is a hip kick, not a knee kick. You should keep your legs and fins under water when doing the flutter kick at the surface. The power in the flutter kick comes from the leg making the downward stroke, while the leg making the upward stroke, or *recovery stroke*, is preparing for the next downward, power stroke. Thus, the power alternates from leg to leg with each kick.

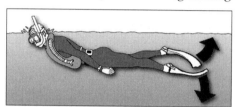

Figure 1-40 The flutter kick.

The *dolphin kick* uses the whole body rather than just the legs (Figure 1-41). The legs are kept together and the body moves in a wavelike motion. To start the dolphin kick, bend the legs at the knees and bring the fins up together while arching the back. Next, straighten the legs and bring them down, while at the same time bending forward at the waist. Think of moving your fins the way a dolphin moves its tail through the water. Focus on the up and down movement of your fins. The action becomes smooth and natural as you gain speed. The dolphin kick has a graceful feel and is fun to experiment with. It's also useful in case you lose a fin. Other kicks depend on two fins, the dolphin works with just one. In fact, to practice the dolphin, take off one of your fins and lay one foot over the other.

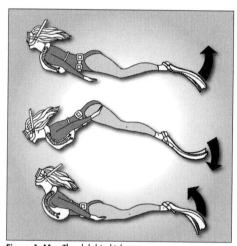

Figure 1-41 The dolphin kick.

The *side scissors kick* is a variation on the flutter kick (Figure 1-42). It is a kick-and-

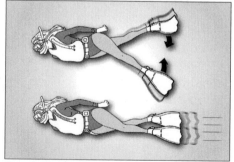

Figure 1-42 The side scissors kick.

glide motion. The body is positioned almost on the side. The legs separate just as with the flutter kick, but on the power stroke the fins are brought together and the diver glides for a few seconds. When the kick is repeated, the legs separate in exactly the same fashion as before—if it is comfortable for the right leg to go high and the left leg low, do it this way every time. The motion of the separated legs coming together is called the *power stroke*, and the position of the fins resting together is called the *glide stroke*. This kick is used primarily in diver rescue techniques.

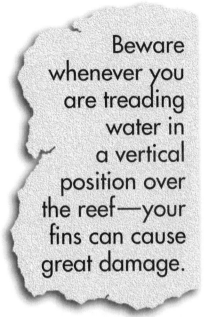

Beware whenever you are treading water in a vertical position over the reef—your fins can cause great damage.

One final note on fin kicks is to beware whenever you are treading water in a vertical position over the reef. Your fins extend well past your feet and can cause great damage to the reef if it is kicked. Always look down to see where you are kicking.

USING THE SNORKEL VEST (BC)

As you swim on the surface, just keep a small amount of air in your vest. This will allow you to relax and explore effortlessly, and will keep your snorkel well above the water level. The snorkel vest also allows you to rest on the surface (Figure 1-43). Unlike the swimmer who needs to keep moving, the snorkeler can stop and totally relax, which is very important in diving.

Figure 1-43   The snorkel vest allows you to rest on the surface.

When you are ready to dive, deflate the vest by pushing the inflate/deflate button and squeezing the vest, or by releasing the air all at once if the vest is equipped with a dump valve.

Do your free dive, and when you return to the surface, clear your snorkel, and stabilize yourself by orally inflating your BC. The method for orally inflating a BC at the surface is called *bobbing* (Figure 1-44). To perform the bobbing technique, kick upward at the surface and inhale, then as you relax and sink back down into the water exhale into the BC through the inflator hose. Then, repeat the process. After a couple repetitions the vest will be inflated enough to allow you to float. If you ever need to inflate immediately in an emergency, some snorkeling vests are equipped

Figure 1-44 The method for orally inflating a BC at the surface is called bobbing.

with a CO_2 cartridge which inflates the vest at the pull of a cord. If you use a cartridge, be sure to replace it before using the vest again.

SURFACE DIVES

After becoming comfortable with your equipment at the surface, you will be ready to try some surface dives. There are two different surface dives: the head-first dive and the feet-first dive. Both use the force of the body to push the diver down into the water, requiring very little energy.

Before doing the dive you'll need to release all the air from your BC.

The *head-first* dive is started from a face down position with the body stretched out on the surface. With a slight forward momentum, bend at the waist so that your upper body forms a right angle to your legs, then lift the legs straight up and out of the water and reach toward the bottom (Figure 1-45). When done correctly the force of the legs will smoothly push your body under without the need to kick. Begin your flutter kick only

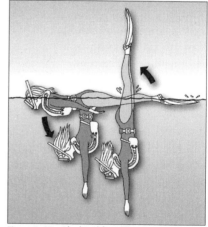

Figure 1-45 The head-first dive.

after your fins have submerged. It does no good for the fins to be used while still above the surface.

The *feet-first* dive is done primarily in kelp beds or where there is limited freedom of movement at the surface. Begin the dive in a floating, vertical position. Separate your legs, one forward and one back, and extend your arms away from your sides. The objective is to lift the body above the surface swiftly, then drop smoothly under. Do this by kicking your legs together forcefully and sweeping your arms down to the sides of your body at the same time. When you're above water, keep your arms at your sides and your legs together forming a "missile" to pierce the water and drop you well below the surface. Once under water, sweep your arms upward to force you further down, then tuck the body, roll forward, and swim down.

In snorkeling, you and your buddy should follow the *one up, one down* system. While one of you dives, the other stays on the surface (Figure 1-46). This is done as a safety measure: The diver on the surface can watch the diver below, and be fresh and ready to assist if that diver should encounter trouble of any kind.

As you ascend, look where you are going and extend an arm above your head to protect against obstructions. When you surface after a free dive, leave your mask on and snorkel in your mouth, move into the face down position, and clear

Figure 1-46   The one up, one down system.

the snorkel, beginning the clear, breathe, and hold method again (Figure 1-47). If you plan on staying on the surface for a while, inflate your BC. If you plan to dive again soon, you can remain buoyant at the surface by keeping your lungs fairly full between breaths.

Figure 1-47   When you surface after a free dive, leave your mask on and snorkel in your mouth, move into the face down position, and clear the snorkel.

EXITS

Always exit the safest and easiest way possible. If you are exiting onto a pool or boat deck, or a raised platform such as a dock, you will need to either remove your fins and lay them on the deck, or hook an arm through the fin straps, if equipped, and climb up. Never climb a ladder wearing fins unless the ladder is designed for this use. If you are making a shore exit, swim or crawl to a place where you can easily stand up and remove your fins, then walk up. Whenever making an exit, keep enough air in your BC to float in case you fall back into the water (Figure 1-48). Shore exits will be covered in depth in Chapter 5.

Figure 1-48   Whenever making an exit, keep enough air in your BC to float in case you fall back into the water.

EQUIPMENT CLEANING, MAINTENANCE, AND STORAGE

MASK, FINS, AND SNORKEL

The mask, fins, and snorkel only require being kept clean and dry. Store these items dry to avoid mildew. Keep all rubber and silicone items out of sunlight when storing. Replace your mask in its protective case.

Maintenance needs might include having to replace a broken mask or fin strap. These are simple operations, though it is important that you match the correct component to your particular model.

EXPOSURE SUITS

There are some general rules for cleaning exposure suits. After using the suit rinse it in clean, fresh water (Figure 1-49). Occasionally the suit should be washed in a wet suit shampoo and lukewarm water. When washing, keep all snaps and zippers open. Make sure you rinse the suit completely. A baking soda rinse will effectively remove odor.

Figure 1-49   After using the suit rinse it in clean, fresh water.

Always hang the suit on wide wooden or plastic hangers in an open, cool, shaded area (Figure 1-50). For long term storage, do not fold the suit. It's fine to cover the suit with a breathable material such as linen to keep dust away. An airtight plastic bag can be used to protect suits against smog; however, the suit must be completely dry. Also, avoid heat and direct sunlight.

Keep zippers and metal fittings lightly lubricated with non-aerosol silicone spray, wax, or bar soap (Figure 1-51). Do not, however, use petroleum based lubricants for fittings on rubber or neoprene components.

Figure 1-50 Always hang the suit on wide wooden or plastic hangers in an open, cool, shaded area.

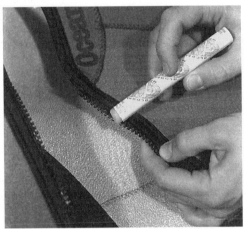

Figure 1-51 Keep zippers and metal fittings lightly lubricated with non-aerosol silicone spray, wax, or bar soap.

SNORKELING VEST: BC

Wash your snorkeling vest in clean, fresh water inside and out. Fill the vest about a third full with water, slosh it around inside, and then empty it. Allow the vest to dry in an open area, then store it out of sunlight, and keep it about half full of air so the insides don't stick together.

BUCKLES

Check the buckles on your weight belt, BC and other equipment to make sure they are neither cracked nor broken and that they operate properly (Figure 1-52). Keep the buckles clean and replace them as needed.

Figure 1-52 Make sure the buckles on your weight belt, BC and other equipment are neither cracked nor broken.

Like any other piece of equipment, the weight belt merely needs to be kept dry and stored in a position which will not twist or bind it. Fasten the belt in a loop for easy handling.

If you are interested in learning more about equipment care and maintenance, you may want to look into taking an *Equipment Techniques* Specialty Course from your local SSI Authorized Dealer

SUMMARY

You may have already noticed that as you complete each phase of your training as a diver you are left wanting more. This is natural. What you are experiencing is fairly predictable: You want to learn and do more!

Snorkeling is a skill that can be exercised by itself, and you will certainly find times when you and your buddy would prefer to do some snorkeling, but by its very nature snorkeling is also a warm-up, a "teaser" for scuba diving. This is your next step: To become a scuba diver. But similarly, scuba is not an end in itself; your desire to experience new diving environments and to learn advanced diving skills will never quite end—once you're hooked!

Scuba DivinG

CHAPTER 2

Chapter 2:
Scuba Diving

So far we've covered the equipment necessary for making the human body more compatible with water. Now we need to address the desire to go under water and explore for extended periods. The most familiar piece of equipment distinguishing the scuba diver from everyone else in the water is the air tank. This and the breathing apparatus called the regulator remedy a biological impossibility for the human body—breathing under water.

In this section we'll reintroduce some of the equipment used for snorkeling, but concentrate on their particular application in scuba diving. Then we'll move on to the equipment which distinguishes the scuba diver from the snorkeler: The *scuba unit,* which consists of the tank, regulator, BC, and monitoring instruments (Figure 2-1, next page).

Scuba equipment that fits well and is compatible with your needs and abilities makes diving more comfortable and enjoyable. Make an appointment to consult with your SSI Dealer or Instructor. They are experts and can help you make the right choices when purchasing equipment.

> Your SSI Dealer or Instructor can help you make the right choices when purchasing equipment.

Figure 2-1   The scuba unit.

SCUBA EQUIPMENT: THE SCUBA UNIT

THE BUOYANCY COMPENSATOR, SCUBA

The weight belt counteracts the positive buoyancy of the diver's body and exposure suit, providing neutral buoyancy which allows the diver to descend; but as the diver descends, increasing pressure compresses the wet suit, eliminating some of its buoyancy while the weight system remains at a constant weight. Tanks become buoyant as air is consumed. Air is added to the BC at depth to counteract the loss of buoyancy (Figure 2-2).

The scuba diver's BC also balances factors such as body weight, various bodies' tendencies toward positive or negative buoyancy, and the relative weight of other equipment being used in order to maintain neutral buoyancy under water.

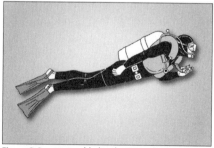

Figure 2-2   Air is added to the BC at depth to counteract the loss of buoyancy.

Like the snorkeler's vest, it can also be inflated at the surface, allowing the diver to float and move around without expending energy. In scuba this is valuable for moving to and from dive sites and surveying dive locations from the surface.

Choosing a Buoyancy Compensator

■ *Jacket Style BCs.* Today's *BC jackets* integrate the scuba tank securing mechanism and harness into their design, making the tank and BC one unit. Jacket style BCs vary in the way the air is distributed around the body. Some distribute the air evenly around the body. Low-profile styles center the air in the bottom of the BC, under the arms, while back-mount styles center the air around the diver's back (Figure 2-3).

Some claim that even air distribution allows the diver to float comfortably in any position. However, others believe that having the air centered under the arms, such as with low-profile styles, allows for less restricted movement and greater comfort, and floats the diver higher above the surface. The back mount BC, however, is preferred by some because it reduces bulk in front of the diver's body.

Figure 2-3   Back-mount BCs center the air around the diver's back, while low-profile styles center the air in the bottom of the BC, under the diver's arms.

■ *Lift.* The amount of *lift*, or how much weight the BC can support at the surface, is determined by the volume of air the BC will hold. This means that warm-water, low-profile BCs, while comfortable, may not provide adequate lift when diving in cold waters with heavy weights and equipment. Conversely, a BC meant to provide a great amount of lift may be bulkier and less comfortable than the warm water diver wants. However, you must choose a BC that has sufficient lift for your body weight. Most manufacturers list the amount of lift each style of BC is designed to provide.

The BC you choose will depend mostly on personal comfort and preference, and the type of environment that you do most of your diving in. Work with your local SSI Dealer and SSI certified Instructor to determine the BC that best suits you.

Buoyancy Compensator Features

■**Inflators.** All BCs are equipped to accommodate an inflator mechanism. The inflation mechanism can inflate the BC either orally or mechanically. Oral inflators consist of a manual control button which opens an air passage through a hose connected to the BC. The button is depressed and the diver blows into a mouthpiece located in the inflation mechanism.

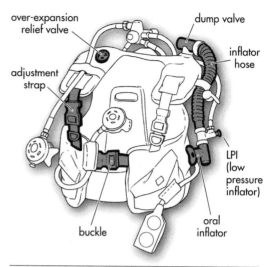

Buoyancy Compensator Features

Power inflators allow you to inflate the BC with air from the tank at the push of a button. Tank air is reduced to a low pressure by design, hence the name *low pressure inflator*, or LPI (Figure 2-4).

■**Deflators.** BCs are deflated in one of two ways. The air can be released slowly by pushing the manual control button on the inflator mechanism (Figure 2-5), or it can be released quickly through a *dump valve*. Dump valves are activated by a pull string, lever, or a release which is controlled by pulling on the inflator hose. When using the manual control button, extend the inflator hose to the highest point in order to get the greatest efficiency in deflation.

A safety feature built into BCs is the *overexpansion relief valve* which is designed to let air vent off when the BC overexpands (Figure 2-6).

■**Inflator-Integrated Air Source.** An important feature which is being seen more and more in newer designs is an alternate breathing apparatus combined with the inflator assembly. This type of alternate air source can eliminate one low pressure hose from the system and replace the conventional octopus regulator (Figure 2-7).

■**Integrated Weight System.** An alternative to the traditional weight belt is the integrated weight system which is built into specially equipped buoyancy compensators (Figure 2-8). These built-in weight systems offer the advantage of reduced bulk in the diver's overall equipment ensemble, and may help reduce back stress.

For safety reasons, divers using integrated weights must learn how to detach the weights quickly. Also, make sure that your buddy becomes familiar with its operation. This can be learned safely by practice in a pool. See your SSI Dealer and your manufacturer's instructions for more information on releasing the weight system.

■ *Other Features.* Jacket type BCs include pockets, and several buckles, belts, and straps both for utility, convenience, and adjustment. A wide cummerbund replaces a standard waist belt on some models, compensating for wet suit compression and expansion and reducing up and down movement of the tank. The tank retaining band is an adjustable nylon strap which buckles to the air tank holding it firmly in place, and can be easily adjusted to accommodate cylinders of varying diameters.

On most models, velcro straps, buckles and other attachments are used to streamline equipment by attaching hoses, lights, instruments, etc. to the BC. Trim all these items as best as you can with the gear you are using (Figure 2-9).

Figure 2-4 Low pressure inflator.

Figure 2-5 Manual control button.

Figure 2-6 Overexpansion relief valve.

Figure 2-7 Alternate breathing apparatus combined with the inflator assembly.

Figure 2-8 The integrated weight system is built into specially equipped buoyancy compensators.

Figure 2-9 Velcro straps, buckles and other attachments are used to streamline equipment.

THE TANK

The tank is the foundation of the sport of scuba diving. Combined with the regulator it forms a self-contained air supply which enables the diver to remain under water untethered.

The tank is relatively simple in design. It is a seamless metal container capable of holding a large amount of compressed air in its relatively small volume. Tanks are regularly available for rent at dive stores, though you will know better what shape it's in and how well it's been maintained if you have your own. Also, having your own would enable you to become familiar with its weight and buoyancy characteristics.

Choosing a Tank

When choosing a tank, realize that the size and construction material of the tank will affect your weighting and buoyancy under water.

■ *Size.* Tank sizes run anywhere from 12 to 190 cubic feet (340 to 5377 liters) (Figure 2-10). The four sizes most common to recreational diving are the aluminum 63 cu.ft. (1783 liters), 80 cu.ft. (2264 liters), 100 cu. ft. (2830 liters) and 120 cu. ft. (3396 liters). The steel 71.4 cu. ft. tank (2021 liters) is also common.

Figure 2-10 Various tank sizes.

Tanks hold air at a maximum of between 2250 and 4,400 pounds per square inch, or psi, (150 and 300 bar). They weigh around 30–40 pounds (13.6–18.1 kg) when empty, and since the weight of the air used is 5-10 pounds (2 to 4.5 kgs), can add up to 5 to 10 additional pounds of buoyancy at the end of the dive.

■ *Materials.* Both steel and aluminum tanks are subject to corrosion; but rust, which forms on the inside of steel tanks, is destructive to the metal, while aluminum oxide, which forms on aluminum, may help to protect the metal from further oxidation. Aluminum tanks will affect your buoyancy more than steel, because there is a greater weight difference between when the tank is full and empty. They are negatively buoyant when full, and positively buoyant when empty. Steel tanks are negatively buoyant and remain so throughout the dive.

Aluminum tanks will affect your buoyancy more than steel.

Tank Valves

Tank valves are threaded and screwed into the tank at the top, but are removed only when the tank is being inspected. Two commonly used valves are the K-Valve and the DIN valve.

■ *K-Valves.* The most commonly used valve in the United States is the K-valve, which is used with the standard yoke first-stage connection. The K-valve has a simple on-off mechanism and is used in tanks with up to 3000 psi (200 bar) working pressure (Figure 2-11).

Figure 2-11   The most commonly used valve in the United States is the K-valve, which is used with the standard yoke first-stage connection.

An important component of the tank valve is the *O-ring.* This small rubber or synthetic ring surrounds the air outlet and provides a seal between the tank and regulator yoke (Figure 2-12). The O-ring is essential to the operation of the breathing system, so it's important to carry extras in case of excessive wear, breakage, or loss.

A safety feature required of all tank valves is the *burst disk.* Air expands when heated, so a tank

Figure 2-12   O-ring.

exposed to heat can become overpressurized. The burst disk prevents explosion by employing a thin metal or teflon disk which ruptures somewhere between 125 and 165 percent of a tank's stamped working pressure, thereby venting excess air in a controlled manner. Older style valves with fusible lead plugs should be upgraded by your SSI Dealer. A valve without the current style burst disk feature can be dangerous.

■ *DIN-Valves.* The DIN valve, which stands for *Deutsches Institute for Normung,* is used on tanks with a working pressure over 3000 psi, which is higher than the standard air pressure allowed in the United States by the Compressed Gas Association (Figure 2-13). While the DIN valve was originally used in Europe it has become popular in the United States, with U.S. manufacturers now designing and selling the valves. Regulator DIN conversion kits are also available which allow for removal of the standard regulator yoke connection and installation of the DIN

Figure 2-13 The DIN valve is used on tanks with a working pressure over 3000 psi.

screw-in connection. It is recommended that a DIN valve be installed by a certified technician. A DIN valve requires a DIN fitting on the regulator.

Tank Features

■ *Markings.* Scuba tanks must conform to government standards. In the United States all tanks have a set of markings stamped on the neck. Tanks without the correct markings are illegal, and reputable dive stores and air stations will not fill tanks which are not marked correctly.

ALUMINUM TANK MARKING DEFINITIONS

(TC)(3ALM)(207BAR)⌐ *Working Pressure*
(DOT)(3AL)(3000)(P417814)(LUXFER)(03A97)(S-80)
⌐*Serial Number*⌐ ⌐*Tank*⌐ ⌐*Tank Size*⌐
⌐*Material Specifications*⌐ *Manufacturer* *in Cubic Feet*
⌐*Governmental Regulatory Agency*⌐ ⌐*Manufacturer Date & Logo*⌐

STEEL TANK MARKING DEFINITIONS

⌐*Governmental Regulatory Agency*⌐ ⌐*Exemption Number*⌐ *Date of Manufacture*
⌐*Working Pressure*⌐
(C)(DOT)(E9791)(3500)(TP5250)(3-97)
⌐*Test Agency*⌐(648652)(PST)⌐*Test Pressure*⌐(3⌂02)
⌐*Serial Number*⌐ ⌐*Tank Manufacturer*⌐ ⌐*1st Test Date & Logo*⌐

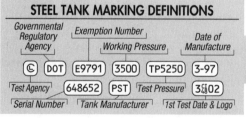

Tank Markings

■ *Tank Boots.* The tank boot is a plastic or hard rubber cap which fits over the bottom of the tank (Figure 2-14). Boots serve two basic functions: They protect surfaces on which the tank is set, and they allow the tank to stand upright while the diver assembles and disassembles the scuba unit. (It is recommended that the tank not be left standing upright when unattended.) Some tank boots are enclosed, which can cause corrosion. Others have built-in drain vents. Some are round and others are hex-shaped which helps prevent the tank from rolling.

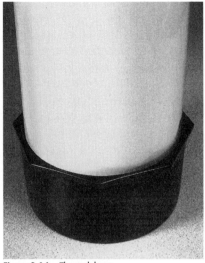

Figure 2-14 The tank boot.

THE REGULATOR

While the tank successfully brings an air supply under water, the regulator is what allows the diver actually to use that high pressure air. Air compressed to 3000 psi (200 bar) certainly cannot be breathed "straight," so the regulator reduces that tank pressure to a breathing pressure (Figure 2-15). Also, a constant air flow would waste air and make exhaling inconvenient, so the regulator compensates for this by supplying air to the diver on demand only when inhal-

Figure 2-15 The regulator reduces tank pressure to a breathing pressure.

ing, and allowing exhaled air to escape through an exhaust valve—the diver breathes both in and out through the regulator mouthpiece.

Choosing a Regulator

A primary consideration for the diver is how easily the regulator "breathes" at depth. Some work more smoothly than others, and therefore cut down on breathing resistance.

Exertion, fatigue, depth, getting chilled, sharing air, and low tank pressure all create additional demand on the regulator, and affect the ease of breathing. Regulators are designed to deliver air on demand. As the diver inhales, air is allowed to flow to the diver. Regulators automatically adjust to increased pressure (ambient pressure) and deliver air to the diver on demand, via the second-stage, at a pressure equal to ambient pressure.

Regulators have two separate mechanisms: the *first-stage* and the *second-stage*. The first-stage reduces the tank pressure to an intermediate pressure around 140 psi/10 bar above ambient pressure (the pressure that surrounds you at any given depth); the air then travels through a hose to the second-stage which is held in the diver's mouth (Figure 2-16). Here the air is essentially stopped and is available to the diver only on demand. When the diver inhales, the air pressure is reduced a second time to equal ambient pressure. Intermediate pressure is also used for BC inflation and dry suit inflation.

> Regulators are designed to deliver air on demand. As the diver inhales, air is allowed to flow to the diver.

In order to make educated choices about regulators, you need a fundamental understanding of how they work.

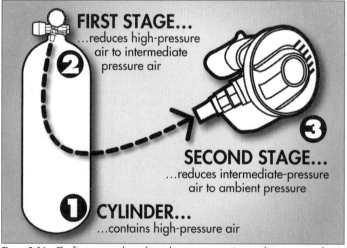

FIRST STAGE...
...reduces high-pressure air to intermediate pressure air

2

3

SECOND STAGE...
...reduces intermediate-pressure air to ambient pressure

1 **CYLINDER...**
...contains high-pressure air

Figure 2-16 The first-stage reduces the tank pressure to an intermediate pressure; the air then travels through a hose to the second-stage which is held in the diver's mouth.

The First-Stage

The first-stage of the regulator attaches to the tank. The purpose of the first-stage is twofold: reduce tank pressure to an intermediate pressure, and keep that pressure as constant as possible as the diver descends and ascends and surrounding pressure varies.

There are two basic designs: the *diaphragm* and the *piston*. Each can have internal mechanisms which are *balanced* or *unbalanced*. Balanced first-stages are slightly more expensive and are usually higher quality, but over the years, the performance gap between balanced and unbalanced first-stages is closing. A balanced first-stage is designed to maintain excellent breathing performance all the way down to very low tank pressure, while some unbalanced units will become harder breathing at greater depths and at tank pressures below 600 or 700 psi (41 to 48 bar).

The *balanced piston first-stage* is designed with few moving parts. Inside the first-stage is a hollow, spring-loaded piston. The piston is exposed directly to the water which allows the regulator to compensate for pressure changes as the diver ascends and descends. As the diver inhales and exhales, the piston unseats and seats itself, releasing and blocking the flow of air (Figure 2-17).

With the *diaphragm, balanced first-stage*, changes in water pressure are transmitted to the valve through a flexible rubber disk which is called a diaphragm. As the diver inhales and exhales, the diaphragm flexes, causing the first-stage valve to open and close (Figure 2-18). The style of first-stage that you choose should be based on the type of diving you plan to do, your budget and your personal preference.

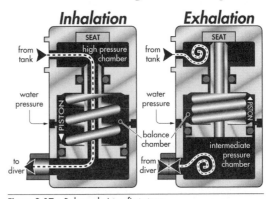

Figure 2-17 Balanced piston first-stage.

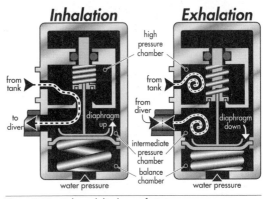

Figure 2-18 Balanced diaphragm first-stage.

The Second-Stage

The second-stage works similar to the first-stage, but reduces intermediate hose pressure to a more breathable ambient level. Air from the hose is let into the second-stage through a small valve. Most all valve mechanisms manufactured today are designed to open with the flow of air (downstream valve). The downstream valve is very efficient, and also best illustrates how the second-stage works (Figure 2-19).

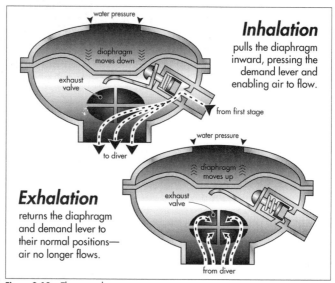

water pressure

Inhalation

pulls the diaphragm inward, pressing the demand lever and enabling air to flow.

diaphragm moves down

exhaust valve

from first stage

to diver

water pressure

diaphragm moves up

Exhalation

returns the diaphragm and demand lever to their normal positions— air no longer flows.

exhaust valve

from diver

Figure 2-19 The second-stage.

The second-stage is held in the diver's mouth with a silicon or rubber mouthpiece. Inside the second-stage is an air chamber, and on the outside of that chamber is a round rubber diaphragm. Touching the inside of the diaphragm is a lightweight lever, and the other end of this lever is attached to the valve controlling the flow of air from the first-stage.

When the diver inhales, the flexible diaphragm is pulled inward. This presses the lever, lifting the valve from its seat and letting air in from the hose. When the diver stops inhaling, the diaphragm returns and the lever and valve assembly shuts off the air. The diver's exhaled air then escapes through a one-way exhaust valve which is located either on the bottom or side of the second-stage.

Like the first-stage, the second-stage also compensates for increasing ambient pressure. As pressure increases, water pushes against the diaphragm, reducing the effort it takes for the diver to pull it inward upon inhaling.

The diaphragm also functions as a *purge valve* at the second-stage. By depressing the purge button on the outside of the mouthpiece with your fingers, the diaphragm is manually pushed inward (Figure 2-20). This allows air to enter the second-stage and clear water from inside the mouthpiece, and also to vent off air before removing the regulator from the tank.

Figure 2-20   The diaphragm also functions as a purge valve.

The regulator has undergone many years of evolution. Improvements in design have made it easier than ever for the diver to breathe under water. Besides performance, the main differences you'll find in regulators are in the quality and durability of their components and materials, in their serviceability, and in their warranties. Your SSI Dealer can help you select the best regulator for your particular needs and budget (Figure 2-21).

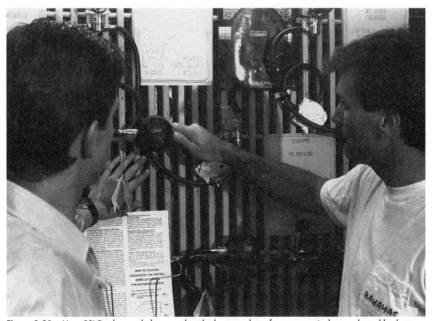

Figure 2-21   Your SSI Dealer can help you select the best regulator for your particular needs and budget.

ALTERNATE AIR SOURCES

In addition to the primary regulator, all scuba units should include a second air source for safety. This alternate air source comes into play in the unlikely event of the primary second-stage failing, or for any reason you and your buddy need to share air. (There is no excuse for running out of air. Divers are equipped with a gauge they can monitor air supply with. You should always plan to return to the surface with no less than 500 psi tank pressure remaining.) Emergency air sharing would then be initiated using this secondary source. Several design options are available.

The *double second-stage*, or "octopus," as it is commonly known, simply utilizes two hoses and two second-stages which run off the same first-stage (Figure 2-22).

Another option is the *independent air system.* This is a small reserve air tank with its own regulator and a supply sufficient for a return to the surface (Figure 2-23 a & b).

Figure 2-22 The double second-stage, or "octopus."

Some alternate air sources are integrated into the BC. The *inflator-integrated air source* is an extra second-stage built right into the buoyancy compensator inflator hose, or integrated into the inflator hose's power inflator mechanism (see Figure 2-7, page 41).

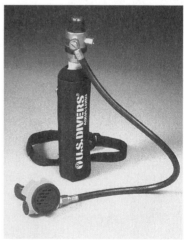

Figure 2-23a   **Figure 2-23b**

Independent air systems.

INSTRUMENTS

By now you are fully equipped to dive. But being able to go under water and stay under water says nothing about the *activity* of diving. You'll be in an environment in which your senses and physiology are altered and somewhat restricted. You must keep track of these subtle changes to avoid problems. You must continuously monitor time, depth, direction, and air supply. Various information instruments allow you to monitor all these things, and help ensure you have an enjoyable experience. In later chapters, you'll come to better understand the importance of having, and using, these valuable instruments.

Analog vs. Digital Instruments

Most instruments are one of two types: *analog* (mechanical) or *digital* (electronic).Various gauges can be separate, but are also available in a *console*—a convenient housing which keeps several gauges together in one easily accessible source.

■ *Analog Instruments.* Analog instruments can be purchased separately as your budget allows, starting with a submersible pressure and depth gauge, and adding a compass, timing device, or computer later (Figure 2-24).

Figure 2-24   Analog instrument.

■ *Digital Instruments.* Electronic gauges are generally more accurate and require less maintenance than analog gauges, plus they can integrate many functions into one unit. Some instruments combine the function of the depth gauge and dive timer, and even the diving computer into one compact unit. These digital units can either be combined with analog instruments in a console, or may come as a wrist unit (Figure 2-25).

If the digital console also combines the function of the submersible pressure gauge then the unit must connect to the first-

Figure 2-25   Digital instruments.

stage of the regulator in some way. The unit can either use a hose to attach to the high-pressure port, or it can be hoseless. *Hoseless instruments* use a transmitter that sends a rapid frequency signal from the regulator first-stage to a receiver display unit which is usually worn on the wrist or attached to the BC (Figure 2-26).

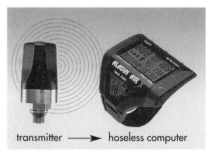

transmitter ———▶ hoseless computer

Figure 2-26 Hoseless instruments use a transmitter that sends a rapid frequency signal from the regulator first-stage to a receiver display unit.

Submersible Pressure Gauge (SPG)

The SPG is the diver's "fuel gauge." It is the instrument most often referred to because it tells the diver how much air remains in the scuba tank (Figure 2-27). The gauge attaches to a high pressure port on the first-stage of the regulator. Some things to look for include large markings and scratch resistant plastic lenses. Gauges are available in English and metric units. The SPG should be referred to continually throughout the dive.

Figure 2-27 The SPG is the diver's "fuel gauge."

Depth Gauge

Knowing your depth is important in adhering to your dive plan. You need to know when you have reached a targeted depth, and monitor your current depth to ensure that planned limits are not exceeded. Most depth gauges are calibrated at feet sea water (FSW) and some are equipped with a maximum depth indicator which records the deepest point reached during a dive (Figure 2-28). Some depth gauges also have altitude compensation.

Figure 2-28 Some depth gauges are equipped with a maximum depth indicator.

The two most popular analog gauges are the oil fill gauge which uses a *bourdon tube*, and the air filled gauge which is activated by a *diaphragm*. These gauges are sealed mechanical devices that react to pressure, which causes the needle to move.

Timing Device

The most prevalent of the timing devices is the dive wristwatch (Figure 2-29). The watch, of course, tells time, but also helps the diver keep track of the time elapsing during a dive. A one-way bezel around the perimeter of the watch face is set at the start of the dive to indicate how many minutes the actual dive has been under way. Digital watches show time and elapsing time automatically with continuous readouts.

Figure 2-29   The most prevalent of the timing devices is the dive wristwatch.

Another timing device is the *dive timer* (Figure 2-30). This instrument is automatically activated by pressure as the diver descends, and stops when the diver returns to the surface, thus showing the total time a diver has spent under water. Dive timers keep track of time spent on the surface between dives as well. Watches should be rated to a depth of at least 100 metres, and better yet, 20 ATMs.

Figure 2-30   Dive timer.

Compass

The compass helps the diver maintain a sense of direction when natural navigation is not possible due to a lack of distinct underwater features or low visibility. It also indicates the way back to an original dive point. There are several styles of compasses.

- **Side-Reading Compass.** This compass either attaches to the wrist or fits in the gauge console and can be read from the top or the side (Figure 2-31a).

- **Top-Reading Navigational Compass.** This compass is designed to plot course headings accurately and to aid in return navigation. It also fits either on the wrist or in a console (Figure 2-31b).

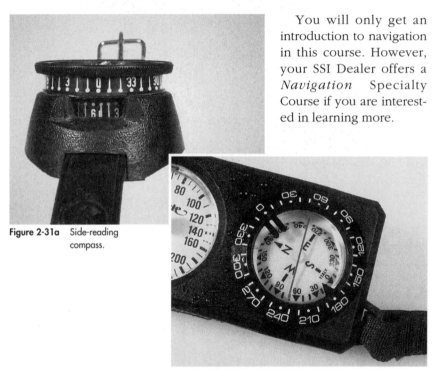

You will only get an introduction to navigation in this course. However, your SSI Dealer offers a *Navigation* Specialty Course if you are interested in learning more.

Figure 2-31a   Side-reading compass.

Figure 2-31b   Top-reading compass.

Dive Computer

The dive computer is more than an instrument. It is a data processor. The type and amount of information the dive computer processes varies between brands and styles (Figure 2-32). All dive computers monitor depth and time while computing your theoretical nitrogen loading. Some also maintain a log of your dives in memory, which includes the dive number, maximum depth, date, time, time remaining and total bottom time. Some incorporate the nitrogen loading bar graph, air consumption indicator, integrated tank pressure, an ascent rate monitor, and even a thermometer and clock.

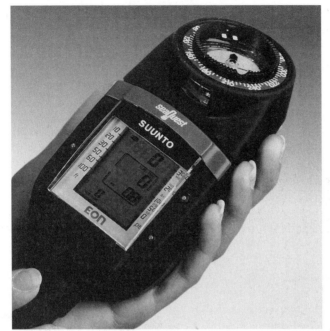

Figure 2-32 The type and amount of information the dive computer processes varies between brands and styles.

Caution should be exercised when using a computer because it uses a theoretical model to calculate nitrogen absorption and elimination. A theoretical model can only approximate the average human physiology and your individual physiology could differ from the model. Therefore, training in dive computer theory and proper use is recommended. SSI offers a course in *Computer Diving*. Nitrogen absorption will be discussed in detail in Chapter 4.

USING THE SCUBA EQUIPMENT

You have already taken an important step in your training as a diver by getting to know the pieces of equipment you'll be utilizing when you get in the water. Now to further prepare you, we will cover some basic skills you need to begin mastering. These skills are not difficult but are very important. First of all, you need to know how to use the equipment in order to know how to dive; equipment and skills are inseparable. Plus, knowing these skills will reduce your apprehension about being in the open water for the first time, and practice will make all the difference in becoming a comfortable and confident diver.

ASSEMBLING THE SCUBA UNIT (Figure 2-33, pages 58 & 59)

Part of learning how to use the equipment is learning how to put it together. There is a standard sequence for assembly of the scuba unit. Do it the same way every time to ensure that nothing is ever left out.

1. **Examine the cylinder and valve for overall condition.** Check visual and hydro dates. Open valve gently to clear any possible debris from the opening and then do a quick air sniff. (If there is any odor, don't use that cylinder. Scuba air should be clean, dry, and odorless.) Inspect the O-ring while you're down there (Figure 2-33a). Replace it if it's missing, cut or badly abraded. Turn the cylinder so that the valve opening points away from you (Figure 2-33b).

2. **Attach BC to cylinder, so that the cylinder retaining band buckling mechanism is facing you** (Figure 2-33c). This puts the cylinder between you and the BC. Check buckling mechanism for condition. It should lock solidly and show no stress cracks or distortion. Lift the unit by holding the BC straps in one hand and the cylinder retaining band in the other (Figure 2-33d). The cylinder should not slip. If it does, the retaining assembly needs to be tightened. You may need to wet the retaining band, as nylon tends to stretch when wet.

3. **Remove dust cover from regulator and quickly check the first-stage filter** (Figure 2-33e). It should be grey in color, with no debris present. If it is any color other than grey, or if there is any debris attached to the filter, have the regulator checked and cleared by your SSI Dealer prior to using it to dive. Check the second-stage mouthpiece for any foreign objects. With the first-stage in your left hand and the second-stage in your right, so that the second-stage is routed over the right shoulder of the BC, drop the regulator yoke over the tank valve (Figure 2-33f). Align the first-stage orifice so that it mates into the tank valve opening, then hand-tighten the yoke (Figure 2-33g). Because of the o-ring seal, tightening the yoke by hand is all that is necessary to establish a properly tensioned connection. Attach low-pressure inflator hose to low-pressure inflator (Figure 2-33h).

4. **Before you turn on the air:**

   • **Attempt to exhale through each second-stage.** Unlike inhaling, you should be able to exhale easily (Figure 2-33i). If you can't, the exhaust valve may be stuck shut. You can usually remedy this by immersing the regulator in water to dilute the light adhesive force that has formed between the exhaust valve and the second-stage housing and then attempting to exhale through the regulator again. Once the valve begins to allow easy exhalation, make sure you still can't inhale. This will ensure that the exhaust valve is functioning properly.

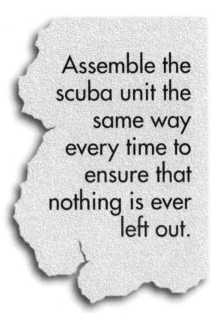

Assemble the scuba unit the same way every time to ensure that nothing is ever left out.

- *Gently attempt to inhale from each second-stage.* If you can inhale, there is a problem with the integrity of the second-stage (Figure 2-33i). Either the diaphragm is holed or the exhaust valves are dislodged or missing. Do not use the regulator until it has been checked and cleared by your SSI Dealer.

- *Check the mouthpieces for condition and proper attachment.* The mouthpiece should be whole (not chewed up!) with no surface cracks evident. Mouthpieces are attached to second-stages with tie wraps. The tie wraps should be in position, tight, and should easily hold the mouthpiece in place even if tugged on.

- *Check the gauges.* Both pressure gauge and depth gauge should register zero at this point in your dive.

5. **Turn gauge face down and away from yourself and others, and slowly pressurize the system**. If you hear a leak, stop and determine the problem. No leaks... open valve all the way (Figure 2-33j). Check pressure gauge to make sure cylinder has adequate air (Figure 2-33k). Do inhale/exhale test again, this time observing pressure gauge. Any fluctuation in the needle indicates an obstruction or a partially closed valve. If the valve is not the problem, have the regulator checked and cleared by your SSI Dealer.

6. **Inflate and deflate BC both orally and manually** to determine proper function of inflator and exhaust valves (Figure 2-33l).

7. **Once the scuba unit is assembled, lay it down** in an easily accessible place or in a special rack provided for that purpose. Be sure to keep the second-stages out of sand or dirt. Leave the unit until you're dressed and ready to dive.

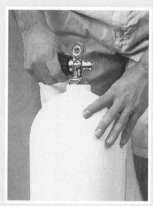

A. Open valve gently to clear any possible debris from the opening and inspect the O-ring while you're there. . . .

B. . . .Turn the cylinder so that the valve opening points away from you.

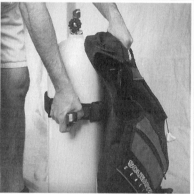

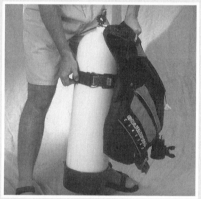

C. Attach BC to cylinder, so that the cylinder retaining band buckling mechanism is facing you . . .

D. . . . Lift the unit by holding the BC straps in one hand & the cylinder retaining band in the other.

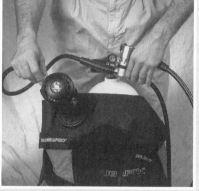

E. Remove dust cover from regulator and quickly check the first-stage filter. . . .

F. With the first-stage in your left hand and the second-stage in your right, so that the second-stage is routed over the right shoulder of the BC, . . .

Figure 2-33 Assembling the scuba unit.

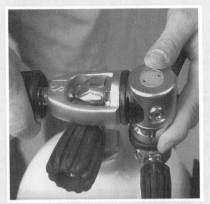

G. . . . Align the first-stage orifice so that it mates into the tank valve opening, then hand-tighten the yoke. . . .

H. . . . Attach low-pressure inflator hose to low-pressure inflator.

I. Exhale and inhale through each second-stage. You should not be able to inhale.

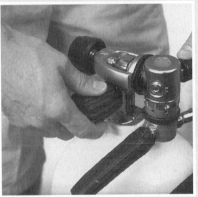

J. Slowly pressurize the system. . . .

K. . . . Check pressure gauge to make sure cylinder has adequate air.

L. Inflate and deflate BC both orally and manually.

DISASSEMBLING THE SCUBA UNIT

When disassembling the unit, follow these steps (Figure 2-34, facing page):

1. **Shut off the tank valve and vent pressure through the second-stage purge valve(s)** (Fig. 2-34a).

2. **Unhook the low-pressure power inflator hose** (Fig. 2-34b).

3. **Unhook any scuba system attachments, i.e., gauge clips, octopus clips, etc.** (Fig. 2-34c).

4. **Remove the regulator yoke** (Fig. 2-34d).

5. **Make sure the dust cap is clean and dry and replace it. To dry, simply shake off the excess water or use a towel** (Fig. 2-34e).

6. **Remove the BC and empty water by inflating it and then holding it up in an inverted position and depressing the deflator button on the inflator hose** (Fig. 2-34f).

7. **Lay the tank down.**

PUTTING ON THE SCUBA UNIT

There are three basic methods for getting into your scuba unit: from a sitting position, from a standing position with help from your buddy, and in the water.

The sitting position is the most convenient but cannot be used in all situations (Figure 2-35). Dive boats are usually equipped with a scuba unit station or platform upon which the diver sets the gear until it's time to dive. The scuba unit is positioned so that the arms can be slipped into it easily from a sitting position. The advantages of this method are that it can be done without help, and that straps can be secured better. While standing, gravity pulls down on the unit; and while in the water, the unit is pushed

Figure 2-35 The sitting position.

and pulled by the water's motion. Putting on the scuba unit from a sitting position can also be done from a bench, or any raised platform big enough for both you and your unit.

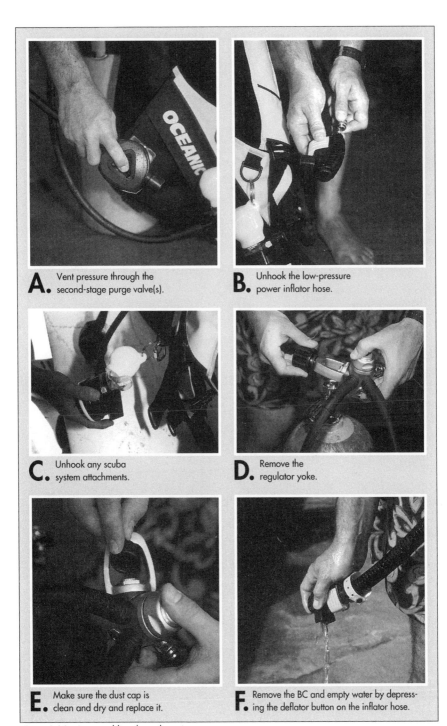

A. Vent pressure through the second-stage purge valve(s).

B. Unhook the low-pressure power inflator hose.

C. Unhook any scuba system attachments.

D. Remove the regulator yoke.

E. Make sure the dust cap is clean and dry and replace it.

F. Remove the BC and empty water by depressing the deflator button on the inflator hose.

Figure 2-34   Disassembling the scuba unit.

The method for donning the scuba unit while standing is called the buddy lift (Figure 2-36). While standing with your back to your buddy, have him or her lift the scuba unit high enough for you to slip your arms into the BC, then hold it there while you make adjustments. The buddy should hold the tank at top and bottom. If one of you is stronger, the stronger buddy should be fitted with the scuba unit first. This is done because it is more difficult for a buddy already encumbered by equipment to lift his or her partner's.

Figure 2-36 The buddy lift.

The method for putting on the scuba unit while in the water will vary according to circumstances. Some dive boats will be equipped with a float line on which the unit will be sent out to the diver (Figure 2-37). The diver's buddy would then assist in putting it on and adjusting it. There are also methods for donning the scuba unit in the water without help.

Regardless of your method of putting on the unit, make sure the BC does not interfere with the weight belt which must be free and positioned for easy ditching.

Figure 2-37 Some dive boats will be equipped with a float line on which the unit will be sent out to the diver.

THE PRE-ENTRY BUDDY CHECK

Gearing up and preparing to enter the water does not consist merely of putting on your equipment. You also need to use the precautionary system called the pre-entry buddy check. You and your buddy will check each other's equipment, assist with adjustments, and generally make sure you are both ready for entry into the water (Figure 2-38).

First, do a visual inspection of your buddy from top to bottom. Is the mask strap in place? Are hoses and gauges routed correctly and kept neatly in place so they won't snag or drag? Is the BC buckled and snug? Is the weight release system accessible? You don't want any equipment left loose or dangling. Loose equipment is susceptible to damage, is difficult to locate under water, and can damage valuable marine life.

Figure 2-38   The pre-entry buddy check.

Next, do a hands-on inspection. Check to see if your buddy's tank valve is open, then look at the pressure gauge to make sure the tank has a sufficient supply of air. Check to see where your buddy's alternate air source is located and that it is properly secured. Also make sure you know how to operate your buddy's weight system.

> ## Don't ever enter the water until "all systems are go."

Your primary concern in doing the pre-entry buddy check is that you are both ready to enter the water. If for any reason you or your buddy are not completely confident that "all systems are go," don't enter the water until you are.

SCUBA ENTRIES

Entry methods for both scuba and snorkeling are identical. However, more complications can arise in entering with full scuba gear because of extra weight and bulk (Figure 2-39). Be aware of your equipment. Make your entry knowing that it will not interfere in any way with the platform from which

Figure 2-39   More complications can arise in entering with full scuba gear because of extra weight and bulk.

you are entering, or with anything in the water, such as a boat ladder or dock pylon. Also, it is even more important in scuba diving than in snorkeling to enter from as stable an area as possible.

You may go under water when entering, so always keep your mask on so you can see, the regulator in your mouth so you can breathe, and the BC inflated so you can float.

USING THE MASK

In scuba, underwater mask clearing is accomplished by gently pushing the top part of the mask against the forehead and exhaling steadily and slowly through the nose while tipping your head back so that you are looking upward (Figure 2-40). The water is pushed out the bottom of the mask. If your mask is equipped with a purge valve, position it at the lowest part of the mask, face downward before purging.

Figure 2-40   Underwater mask clearing.

As you descend, exhale gently through your nose to equalize the pressure inside your mask. Unless pressure inside the mask is increased so that it equals increasing outside pressure, the diver will experience an uncomfortable condition called a *squeeze*.

Ear squeezes are avoided by pinching the nose closed with thumb and index finger, then attempting to gently exhale through the nose (Figure 2-41). This equalizes the middle ear against the force of the water pressing in from the outside. The sensation of equalization is similar to "popping" your ears while driving down a mountain pass or landing in an airplane. The procedures used in those situations— yawning, swallowing, wiggling the jaw—can be used to help equalization along in diving, too.

Figure 2-41   Ear squeezes are avoided by pinching the nose closed with thumb and index finger, then attempting to gently exhale through the nose.

Whatever method or combination of methods you use, be careful not to blow too hard while your nose and mouth are shut off—this can cause injury to the inner ear.

Flexing the eustachian tubes even before you enter prepares them for equalization under water. To avoid problems with equalizing, begin before you descend, as you submerge, and continually as you descend. Never wait for discomfort to occur, but equalize *before* discomfort has a *chance* to occur.

If you have a problem equalizing as you descend, stop, or ascend a few feet until you are successful and the discomfort subsides. Never disregard pain or discomfort. If equalization is not possible, don't dive.

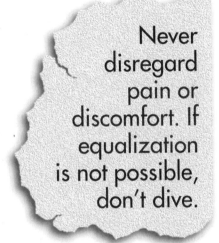

Never disregard pain or discomfort. If equalization is not possible, don't dive.

When the need to replace the mask under water arises, exhale gently through the nose while replacing it, then clear the mask. This will help you avoid getting water up your nose.

USING THE REGULATOR

Breathing with the regulator is easy once you become familiar with it. The method for breathing through a regulator is a slow, steady inhalation followed by a relaxed exhalation. Don't rush. Relax and let the air flow out naturally with each exhale. For reasons that will be explained later, it is important to develop the habit of breathing all the time with a regulator. ***Never hold your breath.*** If the regulator is out of your mouth, teach yourself to exhale a continuous, steady stream of bubbles (Figure 2-42). In addition to knowing how to breathe through it, you need to know how to clear the regulator, and how to retrieve and clear it if for any reason it comes out of your mouth, or if you need to remove it from your mouth in the rare case of air sharing.

Figure 2-42   If the regulator is out of your mouth, teach yourself to exhale a continuous, steady stream of bubbles.

Any time water enters the regulator mouthpiece, you'll need to clear it. The most common way to clear it is to exhale with slightly more force than usual into the mouthpiece, expelling water through the exhaust valve (Figure 2-43). The regulator can also be cleared by pushing the second-stage purge button for a moment. Always inhale cautiously after clearing.

If the regulator second-stage comes out of your mouth while under water, remember first to keep exhaling and not to hold your breath. To retrieve the regulator second-stage, swing your right arm down and to your side and hook the regulator hose from underneath (Figure 2-44a). If you

Figure 2-43 The most common way to clear the regulator is to exhale with slightly more force than usual into the mouthpiece, expelling water through the exhaust valve.

aren't able to locate it immediately, rotate or lean your body slightly to the right so that gravity pulls the second-stage down into view. Another method is to reach over your shoulder for the regulator yoke attached at the tank valve and follow the hose down to the second-stage with your hand (Figure 2-44b). Your buddy can also offer assistance in locating the second-stage. If you cannot locate your primary second-stage, another option is to breathe off your alternate air source until your primary can be located.

Figure 2-44a Swing your right arm down and to your side and hook the regulator hose from underneath.

Figure 2-44b Reach over your shoulder for the regulator yoke attached at the tank valve; follow the hose down to the second-stage with your hand.

When you have the regulator in hand and you're ready to replace it, you'll need to clear it before inhaling again. After clearing, inhale slowly, making sure there is no water left inside the mouthpiece.

Snorkel Use in Scuba Diving

The snorkel is used for only one reason in scuba diving, for preserving tank air while moving around at the surface. Normally, use your snorkel while surface swimming from entry points to points of descent, and from points of ascent to exit points. In surging or choppy water conditions where there is a possibility of inhaling water, such as when exiting on shore with surf, some divers may choose to use the regulator.

USING THE BC

In scuba diving the BC is used in four basic ways: floating at the surface, controlling descents, establishing neutral buoyancy at depth, and aiding in ascents. We will look at how it is used to establish neutral buoyancy and its importance in making ascents more in depth in Chapter 3, but for now we'll look at how to make a comfortable descent by utilizing the BC.

> In scuba diving the BC is used for floating at the surface, controlling descents, establishing neutral buoyancy at depth, and aiding in ascents.

Descending

Unlike a snorkeling dive, the scuba descent needs to be done slowly, and started in an upright position so that the diver can gradually equalize and control the rate of descent in order to avoid impact with the bottom, or to avoid going beyond prescribed depth limits (Figure 2-45). To start your descent, begin in a feet-first position, hold the inflator hose above your head in your left

Figure 2-45 The scuba descent needs to be done slowly, and started in an upright position.

hand, and let air escape the BC by depressing the deflate button or pulling down on the inflator mechanism to operate the dump valve. Once the BC is completely deflated, exhale and relax to get yourself under the water. Never help your buddy by pulling him or her under water on descent unless you have been asked to help. Assisting a buddy when he or she is not expecting it can lead to problems!

As you descend, the wet suit will compress due to increasing pressure. As the buoyancy of the wet suit decreases, adding small amounts of air to the BC will help control your descent (Figure 2-46). As you approach the depth at which you would like to stabilize, add more air to the BC, if needed, to become suspended in the water. Be careful not to add too much air, because this will make you positively buoyant and cause you to begin ascending. Your objective is to establish *neutral* buoyancy, a condition of neither sinking nor floating up. Look down periodically as you descend to watch where you are going. This will help you avoid collision with the coral reef or any marine life.

Figure 2-46   As the buoyancy of the wet suit decreases, adding small amounts of air to the BC will help control your descent.

It is a good idea to use a line for both descents and ascents if the environmental conditions and dive site allow for it. Lines allow you to stay with your buddy, better control your rate of ascent and descent, and stop to equalize pressure or handle minor emergencies (Figure 2-47). During your training the Instructor will make the decision whether a line is appropriate. Upon certification, you should consider the value of using a line each time you dive.

Figure 2-47   It is a good idea to use a line for both descents and ascents if the environmental conditions and dive site allow for it.

Ascending and Surfacing

You and your buddy should decide when you want to ascend, then do so together. You should always be neutrally buoyant when starting your ascent. If you are not, add a small amount of air to your BC to achieve neutral buoyancy. Then use a gentle fin kick to begin ascending upward. As you ascend pressure will decrease, and this will cause your BC to become more positively buoyant. This will help you to ascend and will allow you to kick slowly. However, you must be aware of your rate of ascent and use your BC to control it (Figure 2-48). Since the air inside your BC will expand as you ascend and make you increasingly buoyant, depress the deflate button or pull the dump cord and allow some air to

escape as you go up. Keep an eye on your depth gauge and timing device, making sure you do not exceed 30 feet (9 metres) per minute. This means you will ascend at one-half foot per second, so an ascent from 30 feet should take 60 seconds. A good exercise is to measure 30 feet and walk the distance in 60 seconds. This will give you an idea of how slowly you must ascend.

Figure 2-48 Be aware of your rate of ascent and use your BC to control it.

Look up and listen for boats while you ascend, making sure your path is clear (Figure 2-49). Make sure to breathe normally at all times, and pay special attention to breathing normally as you ascend—the lungs can be damaged on ascent if you hold your breath. This is explained in more detail in Chapter 3. Again, on any ascent, do not try and assist your buddy unless you have been asked to help. Assisting your buddy when it is not expected can lead to problems.

Figure 2-49 Look up and listen for boats while you ascend, making sure your path is clear.

When you surface, leave your mask on and your regulator in your mouth, and inflate your BC. After stabilizing, you can change to snorkel breathing to save tank air.

DITCHING THE WEIGHT SYSTEM

You have already learned how to establish proper weighting using the weight system in Chapter 1 and we will discuss it further in Chapter 3, but there is another important role for the weights, specifically as combined with the buoyancy characteristics of the BC and wet suit.

A skill you'll need to know in case you ever have to make an emergency buoyant ascent, or need additional emergency surface buoyancy, is *weight ditching*. If using a belt, first locate it using the *quick draw* method: Bring your hands to your thighs and then move them upward until you locate the belt (Figure 2-50 a & b). Then move your hands along the belt to locate the weights. Even if the belt has shifted and the buckle is no longer in front, by finding the weights and moving from them toward the center of the belt you will be able to locate the buckle (Figure 2-50c). Unbuckle the belt and hold it out to your side at arm's length so that it can't interfere with other equipment, then drop it (Figure 2-50d). If you are under water, you will be able to make a direct non-stop ascent. If you're on the surface, you will be buoyant.

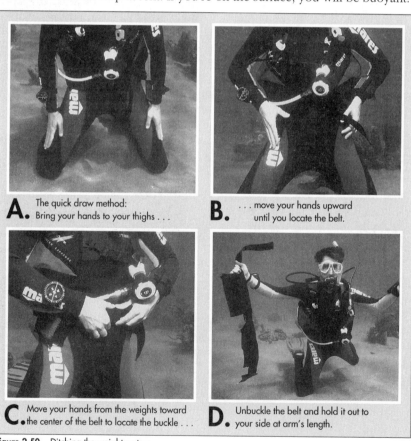

A. The quick draw method: Bring your hands to your thighs . . .

B. . . . move your hands upward until you locate the belt.

C. Move your hands from the weights toward the center of the belt to locate the buckle . . .

D. Unbuckle the belt and hold it out to your side at arm's length.

Figure 2-50 Ditching the weight system.

SCUBA EXITS

As with entries, your primary concern in exiting the water is doing it the safest and easiest way possible. Variations on exiting are based on environmental factors and the kind of diving you're doing. As a general rule, when exiting leave your equipment in place and your BC inflated until you are safely out of the water. Be sure to have an exit point and exit method planned even before entering the water.

Boat Exits

If you are exiting the water onto a boat, the method will depend mostly on the boat captain or dive leader's preference (Figure 2-51). They may advise you either to remove your fins and climb up, or remove equipment while in the water and hand it up first. If you are removing equipment in the water, start with the weight belt.

Figure 2-51   If you are exiting the water onto a boat, the method will depend mostly on the boat captain or dive leader's preference.

Though some methods will differ, there are a few general rules to follow: Never climb a ladder with fins on, unless the ladder is designed for this use; make sure there is air in your BC when you take it off in water; always assist your buddy in maintaining stability and removing and handing up equipment.

Shore Exits

When making an exit in calm water conditions and on a shore with a gradual incline, such as a sandy beach, you and your buddy should swim together to a place where you can safely help each other remove your fins, then stand and walk up onto the beach (Figure 2-52). In surf, or in an area where there is some sort of abrupt approach to the beach such as a ledge, allow the water to bring you shoreward as far as possible, then crawl to a point at which it is safe to remove fins and walk up.

Figure 2-52   When making an exit on a shore that has a gradual incline, swim together to a place where you can safely help each other remove your fins, then stand and walk up onto the beach.

ACCESSORIES, AND EQUIPMENT MAINTENANCE

DIVING ACCESSORIES

The equipment covered so far consists of the basics. When you know how to use them, you'll essentially know how to dive. In addition to the basics, there are some accessories which can further help you become a safer and more confident diver.

Flags and Floats

It's hard for boaters to see divers on the surface, and it would be impossible for boaters to know when divers are under them if not for a system of communicating these facts. The diver's flag and dive boat flag serve this purpose. However, caution must still be exercised because some boaters are unaware of the meaning of these flags.

The two kinds of flags used are the *recreational diver's flag* and the *alpha flag*, or the international "diver down" flag. The recreational diver's flag is red with a diagonal white stripe (Figure 2-53). It says, "There are divers below; keep clear, and travel at slow speed." It is flown only when divers are actually in the water. The recreational diver's flag is governed by tradition, and in some places by law. Your SSI Dealer will know the rules in your area.

Diver's flags are displayed on some sort of float. This could be a buoy, lifesaver, inner tube, surfboard, or small raft. Larger rafts and boats make good floats in deep water situations or on repetitive dives, because you can store equipment in them or use them in emergencies.

The alpha flag is blue and white with a "V" cut into one side (Figure 2-54). It is flown from boats and says, "This vessel has divers below and maneuverability is restricted." It is often used during commercial dives when divers are tethered to the boat by hoses or lines. The alpha flag is the dominant flag used in international and inland navigable waterways.

Figure 2-53 The recreational diver's flag is red with a diagonal white stripe.

Figure 2-54 The alpha flag is blue and white with a "V" cut into one side.

Signaling Devices

It is extremely important that you and your buddy maintain contact at all times and never lose track of each other's location. But if you do lose your buddy, or you surface some distance from the shore or boat, you may want to use a signaling device to attract attention. However, use it as a last resort, as it is an *emergency* signal and will undoubtedly alert others nearby that there is something wrong. Signaling devices are used because they work much better than shouting, can be more easily seen or heard over the waves and wind, and they take less energy. Also, some signaling devices are specifically designed for use under water.

- **Whistles and Alarms.** (Figure 2-55). Plastic whistles and other audible signaling devices such as alarms work well for signaling on the surface. Attach them to your BC inflator hose or other easily accessible place.

Figure 2-55 Whistles and alarms.

- **Signal Flares.** The day/night flare can be used to signal an emergency, or to communicate a diver's whereabouts to a boat crew or a party on shore. The red flare is for emergencies, and the white flare is for location.

- **Inflatable Surface Marker.** Surface markers are available that fit in your BC pocket, and can be inflated on the surface with your regulator second-stage. These devices extend 4 or more feet (1.2 metres) above the water so you can attract attention on the surface (Figure 2-56).

- **Underwater Audible Devices.** There are a variety of devices on the market that make noise under water to attract your buddy's attention. These devices vary from a plastic ball that bangs on your tank, to

Figure 2-56 Surface markers extend 4 or more feet (1.2 metres) above the water so you can attract attention on the surface.

sophisticated alarms. Ask your SSI Dealer what types of underwater signaling devices are available.

Underwater Lights

The most common illuminating device is the battery powered or rechargeable battery underwater light. These are waterproof flashlights with varying degrees of durability and candle power. The rechargeable type is more expensive, but could save you money in the long run by eliminating the cost of buying batteries. However, you must remember to recharge the batteries after use. Follow manufacturer's recommendations for recharging. Lights come in a variety of sizes from the personal locator light, which attaches to the tank valve or to the diver, to narrow beam and wide beam flashlights (Figure 2-57). More information on lights can be obtained from your SSI Dealer, or from a *Night/Limited Visibility Diving* Specialty Course.

■ ***Chemical Glow Light.*** It is constructed of a small glass inner tube containing one chemical, and a larger plastic outer tube containing another. When you bend the plastic tube, the tube inside breaks and the chemicals mix, creating a bright glow. The light usually attaches to the diver's tank valve or to the diver as a way for buddies to keep track of each other at night or in limited visibility. However, they should not be used instead of a light, or as a back-up light. After use, the lights should be properly discarded and not left in the water or on the shore.

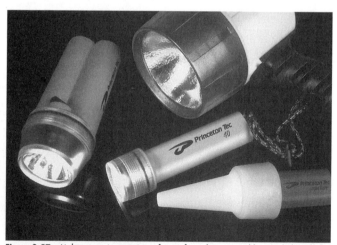

Figure 2-57 Lights come in a variety of sizes from the personal locator light, which attaches to the tank valve or to the diver, to narrow beam and wide beam flashlights.

Dive Knives

The dive knife is a tool and not often used, but when you need it, it can be very handy, and in some cases a life saver. Most commonly the knife fits into a sheath attached at an easily accessible place, such as the inside of the diver's lower leg or the BC (Figure 2-58 a & b). It can be used to free yourself if you become ensnared while under water, and to tap on your tank to get a buddy's attention. The knife should be made of non-corrosive metal, and should be strong and sharp. It is recommended that the metal of the knife extend all the way through the handle. Make sure that local laws or rules allow you to have and carry a dive knife when diving.

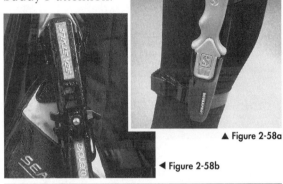

▲ Figure 2-58a

◄ Figure 2-58b

Most commonly the knife fits into a sheath attached at an easily accessible place, such as the inside of the diver's lower leg or the BC.

DiveLogs

Your SSI DiveLog is an important accessory used for recording dive statistics such as temperatures at certain depths, visibility, underwater features, and what type of equipment and weights were used on the dive. This information can be helpful in planning future dives and remembering past dives (Figure 2-59).

Figure 2-59   Your SSI DiveLog is an important accessory.

Another key function of the SSI DiveLog is to track your continuing education and your number of logged dives. Both are valuable and rewarded with the SSI system. All of your logged dives count toward advanced ratings such as *Advanced Open Water Diver* and *Master Diver,* plus you can receive recognition stickers and cards just for logging dives. Work towards your Century Diver, Gold 500 Diver or Platinum 1000 Diver cards. These prestigious cards were the first in the industry to recognize divers just for diving.

Thermometers

The thermometer is another valuable piece of equipment in recording dives. You can record temperatures at particular dive sites so that variations in features (algae, visibility) affected by temperature or your exposure suit needs can be predicted. Many new digital gauges and dive computers come with a built-in thermometer.

Spare Parts and Repair Kit (Figure 2-60)

It would be a shame to have to call off a dive because of something as simple as a broken mask strap. A small kit containing essential spare parts and some basic tools such as pliers, a crescent wrench, allen wrenches, and a screw driver should always be taken along. Make certain that the items you carry are appropriate replacement parts for your specific pieces of diving equipment. Mask and fin straps are not necessarily generic. See your SSI Dealer for consultation. Include at least these items:

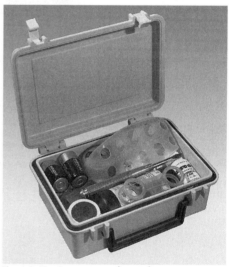

Figure 2-60   Spare parts and repair kit.

- ■ Fin strap and buckle
- ■ Mask strap and buckle
- ■ An assortment of O-Rings
- ■ Snorkel keeper
- ■ Anti-fogging solution
- ■ Non-aerosol Silicone spray
- ■ Wet suit cement or patches
- ■ Waterproof plastic tape

- ■ Needle and thread
- ■ Small first aid kit and booklet
- ■ Extra batteries for lights, watches and digital gauges
- ■ Regulator mouthpiece
- ■ Regulator first-stage port plugs
- ■ Tie wraps

For travel to remote dive destinations you may want to carry an extra mask, and extra high and low pressure hoses. Other items you might consider have to do with your personal equipment, such as a camera system.

Equipment Bags

By now you realize the extent to which equipment plays a role in diving. This volume of equipment necessitates a place to put it all. Your equipment bag should be big enough and strong enough to hold everything except the tank and weight belt (Figure 2-61). It should be made of durable material and should have heavy duty zippers, handles, and seams so it is easy to travel with.

Once at the dive site, a mesh bag capable of holding your gear should be used (Figure 2-62). On boats and at tropical dive destinations, equipment will constantly be getting wet, and will stay wet due to the humidity. A mesh bag allows air to reach the equipment so it can dry, which helps keep the equipment from smelling and molding. It also serves to keep your personal equipment together on boats and separate from others' equipment. Some items look very similar and mix-ups can easily occur.

Figure 2-61 Your equipment bag should be big enough and strong enough to hold everything except the tank and weight belt.

Figure 2-62 Once at the dive site, a mesh bag capable of holding your gear should be used.

EQUIPMENT CLEANING AND MAINTENANCE

Buoyancy Compensator

After the dive, drain the BC of any water that has entered through the inflator hose. Then rinse the BC inside and out with clean, fresh water. To rinse the inside, fill it through the inflator hose about one-third with water, then inflate it and slosh the water around (Figure 2-63a). It is recommended that you drain the water through an exhaust valve. If this is not possible you may need to drain the water by inverting the BC and holding the inflator hose down with the oral inflator open (Figure 2-63b). Make sure push buttons and inflator components are clean and clear of silt or impurities. BCs drain best when they are fully inflated.

When storing the BC, allow it to dry in an open area, and leave it half full of air to keep the insides from sticking together.

You can check for leaks in the BC by filling it with air and submersing it in a bathtub and watching for bubbles. If it does leak, it should be taken to your dive store for professional repair. Check with your owner's manual to see how often your BC should be serviced.

Figure 2-63a To rinse the inside of the BC, fill it through the inflator hose about one-third with water.

Figure 2-63b Drain the water by inverting the BC and holding the inflator hose down with the oral inflator open.

Regulator

Make sure the dust cap is clean and dry before replacing it. Flush the mouthpiece and exhaust port with clean, fresh water (Figure 2-64). It is important not to let any water into the regulator hose. To avoid water contamination of the inside of the regulator hoses, never push the purge valve while rinsing the inside of the second-stage.

Do not hang the regulator by the hose when storing. This can permanently bend the hose and weaken it at the point of the bend. Gently wind the hoses into a storage bag to prevent damage and keep out dust. Hose protectors can be added where the hose meets the first-stage of your regulator to protect your hoses from excess wear (Figure 2-65).

All repairs to the regulator should be done by your SSI Dealer, and it is a good idea to have them serviced annually, or as often as is recommended by your owner's manual. Record maintenance of your scuba equipment in the Equipment section of your SSI DiveLog (Figure 2-66).

Instruments

As with the regulator, rinse the instruments and store them clean and dry. Do not allow water inside the hose, and when storing, don't hang it by the hose. Check your owner's manual to see how often they recommend you have your instruments serviced. You will also need to periodically have the bat-

Figure 2-64   Flush the mouthpiece and exhaust port with clean, fresh water.

Figure 2-65   You can protect your hoses from excess wear by adding hose protectors.

SSI EQUIPMENT MAINTENANCE

EQUIPMENT:_____

Brand: _____
Model: _____
Serial #: _____
Purchase Date: _____
Dealer: _____
Salesperson: _____

DATE	TECH'N	SERVICE PERFORMED	COMMENTS

Figure 2-66   Record maintenance of your scuba equipment in the Equipment section of your SSI DiveLog.

teries in digital instruments changed. Many digital instruments can only be serviced by the manufacturer. This may also include replacement of the batteries. It is impossible to purchase some of these specialized batteries in remote dive destinations. Periodic accuracy checks can be done at your SSI Dealer. During periods of extended (one week or more) storage and while traveling, remove batteries from devices.

Tank

The safe and efficient operation of the tank depends on proper maintenance and inspection. Like any other piece of equipment, it should be kept clean and dry, but there are additional, specific steps you must take in order to keep the tank safe and working properly.

■ *Storing and Transporting the Tank.* Never store a tank empty. It is recommended that some air pressure remain in the tank. This will prevent moisture from getting in, or from forming because of temperature changes. It is recommended that tanks be stored lying down whenever possible. Any time a tank is stored, it should be well secured and kept away from children.

Secure the tank during transport in an automobile by laying it down lengthwise on the floor, trunk, or truck bed with the valve end toward the rear. Wrap the valve with thick padding and tie the tank down or block it so that it cannot easily move, even if jolted (Figure 2-67). Also, keep it out of direct sunlight and avoid prolonged storage in a place which may overheat.

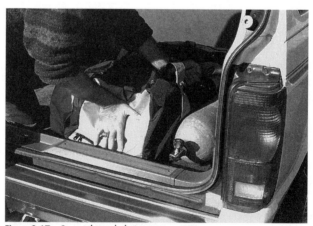

Figure 2-67   Secure the tank during transport.

■ *Preventing Damage to the Tank.* To prevent interior moisture and contamination is to make sure tank fittings, openings, and O-rings are dry before scuba unit assembly.

There are some precautions you can take periodically to make sure your tank is dry and uncontaminated inside. Follow the rule of "look and feel, smell, and listen" (Figure 2-68):

1. **Look and Feel.** Turn the valve on and watch the air as it comes out. Damp air is white. Dry air is invisible. Also, feel the stream of air, and rub your fingers to see if any moisture has escaped the tank.

2. **Smell.** If the air smells damp or metallic, there could be water, oil, or rust inside. Pure air does not have an odor.

Figure 2-68 To make sure your tank is dry and uncontaminated inside, follow the rule of "look and feel, smell, and listen."

3. **Listen.** While turning the tank upside-down, listen for loose particles and water. Any rattling could signal that there are rust chips or other impurities inside. If you suspect anything, take the tank to your SSI Dealer for a professional T.I.P.® inspection.

■ **T.I.P.® (Tank Inspection Program).** Always have a T.I.P.® done at least once a year, or more frequently with heavy use, by your dive store. This visual inspection will determine whether there is any contamination inside, and will assess the general condition of the tank. The inspection starts with looking the tank over for obvious flaws such as dents or stripped threads, then checking the interior for contaminants or corrosion.

■ **Hydrostatic Testing.** In the U.S. a tank must be hydrostatically tested every five years. In other countries this varies, and can be as frequent as every year. The hydrotester must be licensed and have current authorization from the proper governmental control agency.The hydrostatic test measures the elasticity of the tank's metal chamber. If the tolerance is exceeded, the metal of the tank is considered fatigued and the tank must be condemned.

Caution: A tank which fails a hydro-test could pass a second test because it has already been expanded. In this case a second opinion could be misleading. The tank is condemned after failing a hydro-test and must not be used again.

SUMMARY

Diving is an enjoyable activity once you begin to get comfortable with the necessary techniques and equipment. We stated earlier that "ability equals comfort, and comfort equals enjoyment." The better you become at handling and making proper use of the equipment, the more comfortable you will become as a diver. Work with your local SSI Dealer and Instructor in determining your needs, and acquire your own equipment as soon as you can. We recommend that you get outfitted while still in training so you can use your equipment under the supervision of your Instructor. You will also be much more comfortable when you do your open water dives. Once you have your equipment, your dive store will also help you maintain it, inspect and repair it, and will fill your air tank. Also see your retailer about new developments in equipment, and the proper techniques for using new items. This will be especially necessary as you progress into advanced courses that depend on equipment, such as computer diving and dry suit diving. Your SSI Dealer and Instructor are equipment experts. Consult them any time you have questions or need advice on purchasing or maintaining equipment (Figure 2-69).

Figure 2-69   Your SSI Dealer and Instructor are equipment experts. Consult them any time you have questions or need advice on purchasing or maintaining equipment.

Get to know your equipment: practice with it and keep it clean and well organized. When using your equipment starts to become second nature, your enjoyment of recreational diving will really take off. Soon you'll be diving right along with the other welcome members of the underwater world.

Adapting the Body to Water and Pressure

Chapter 3:
Adapting the Body to Water and Pressure

Have you ever wondered what the lure of diving is? What possesses someone to look forward for months to a diving vacation in the Caribbean, or even to devote his or her life to underwater exploration? Well, just imagine an inner city teenager from New York donning a backpack and ascending to the summit of a 14,000 foot peak in the Rocky Mountains for the first time. A new environment can be a thrill; sometimes enough of a thrill to make you want to stay, or at least visit often.

For the scuba diver that new environment is always nearby, and the experience can be prolonged, repeated, and made a part of your life. What makes diving accessible is that water is always with us, and is everywhere we go; what makes it possible is that the human body can be adapted to function in water almost as well as it does on dry land.

The breathing process maintains life, and anywhere a person can breathe, that person can potentially survive. Breathing under water is your ticket to a new world. The differences between breathing in water and on land are functions of equipment, as we've already covered, and an understanding of the breathing process and how it is affected by water and pressure. In this chapter you'll learn about breathing and how to do it effectively while scuba diving. You'll also learn other methods of adapting to the underwater environment, including maintaining proper buoyancy and following safe procedures for making ascents and descents.

BREATHING UNDER WATER

Breathing is not something we usually pay attention to. It just happens. But under water you become acutely aware of breathing (Figure 3-1).

Your mind and body know you are out of your element and are telling you so. While you can overcome the unfamiliar environment with equipment, you will require knowledge and training to compensate for various physiological differences. You need to know that while gases are exchanged in underwater breathing just as they are on land, pressure changes affect the amounts of those gases and the rates of their exchange.

Before going into the actual physiology of breathing, we'll look at what it takes to breathe efficiently regardless of environment, which can only help you become a better diver.

Figure 3-1 Under water you become acutely aware of breathing.

DIVING FITNESS

Statistics show that diving is not a hazardous activity. There are fewer accidents in diving than skiing, for instance. When accidents *do* occur, they often involve divers who are in some way predisposed to risk. Certain risk factors are environmental, but many are individual. While lack of training, or poor judgement are probably the most common problems, divers who are overweight, smoke, drink heavily, or are generally out of shape may increase their chances of dive-related injury.

Besides helping to ensure personal safety, the healthy individual simply makes a better diver. There are certain practices and precautions that will make the difference in recreational diving being tiring and uncomfortable, or effortless and exciting. Some of these have to do more with short term diving preparation such as getting plenty of sleep and not consuming alcohol the night before a dive, but others are more long term, such as maintaining a good diet, participating in a regular exercise program, and getting regular medical checkups—especially if you...

■ Smoke
■ Are over 45
■ Are overweight
■ Have had recent surgery
■ Are on medication
■ Or have heart, respiratory, or other medical problems that might warrant concern.

Cardiovascular Fitness

Some think diving is relatively non-physical. But although the activity of diving is not high tempo, it is done in the heavy medium of water, requiring strength, and is done for extensive periods, requiring stamina. Just as with skiing, it is a good idea to prepare yourself for "the season."

For diving, it is recommended that the first thing you do is get a medical checkup. After determining that you are in good health, do a little "tuning up" by exercising your heart and lungs. Common aerobic exercises include jogging, cycling, swimming, aerobic dance, and sports in which cardiovascular activity is sustained (Figure 3-2).

Cardiovascular fitness also means increased circulation. This helps keep divers warmer longer, helps them stay alert, which is important in problem solving, and also means less work for the lungs in getting oxygen into the blood, which allows the diver to consume less tank air.

Figure 3-2   Do a little "tuning up" by exercising your heart and lungs.

Healthy Lungs

Efficient lungs are very important to reduced risk in diving. Even very healthy divers can have difficulty because of lung problems, either temporary or chronic. Since divers continually vent the air they breathe, aerobic fitness, again, can help in that it guards against carbon dioxide buildup. But sometimes fitness is not enough.

Anything that restricts breathing, the flow of air out of the lungs, or the exchange of gases in the respiratory system can make certain divers more susceptible to problems. For this reason divers who have colds or flu, have chronic sinus ailments which cause excessive phlegm or blockage of the sinuses or bronchial tubes, or have asthma, should seek the counsel of a dive medicine physician.

One of the most commonly asked questions concerning medical problems and diving is: Can I dive with asthma? The answer to this question is that asthma can cause trapped gas in the small airways of the lungs, and any time this happens under water there is a greater risk of lung expansion injury. Any type of asthma poses this risk, so asthmatics have a much greater risk of dive-related injury. If you have asthma, see a dive medicine physician before attempting to dive.

It is possible to dive while using a medication which helps eliminate the symptoms of an illness or disorder, but it is important to be aware of possible side effects such as drowsiness which in turn may impair judgement. It is also not known at this time what, if any, effects pressure and depth have on the human body while on medication. It is therefore recommended that you either dive only when you are well, or after getting the consent of your physician for using medication while diving (Figure 3-3).

Figure 3-3   Dive only when you are well, or after getting the consent of your physician for using medication while diving.

Of course, a precaution everyone can take to ensure better lung health is not to smoke.

Breath Control: Stress Control

Given healthy lungs, other breathing problems are related to anxiety or fear under water. A common reaction to anxiety or fear is a rapid, shallow breathing pattern. Shallow breathing can then lead to an out-of-breath feeling. The way to avoid the stress, and even panic, which can result from this anxiety and its related uneven breathing pattern is simple: breathe normally.

To control anxiety and stress, and thereby avoid an erratic breathing pattern, first become aware of your anxiety if some difficulty arises, then **stop, breathe normally,** and **think** until you are relaxed and in control. A "difficulty" may be something as simple as an ill-fitting wet suit which restricts movement, gradually making you breathe harder because of extra physical exertion. As with any problem, the solution is to *fix* the problem, not to react to it emotionally. By consciously returning your breathing to normal, and remaining calm and alert,

you can avert stress and allow yourself to respond logically. This is not hard to do. Remember that you are there to enjoy your dive, and if anything interferes with that, take care of it immediately but calmly, and keep breathing normally.

THE FUNCTION OF THE LUNGS

Speaking of the lungs as something isolated inside the body, as we usually do, is not really correct. The lungs are part of a complex system which circulates throughout the body, bringing fuel to the cells and eliminating their waste.

The lungs themselves are made up of clusters of elastic sacs, and are suspended from air tubes. The windpipe connects the throat and the lungs. This pipe splits off in a "Y", sending air into the two separate lungs; the air is brought into the lungs by smaller airways called the bronchial tubes. These lead through smaller and smaller airways to clusters of tiny sacs at the inside of the lung membrane called *alveoli*. Each tiny sac, or *alveolus*, is constructed of blood capillaries and membrane. This is where the transfer of gases in and out of the blood takes place (Figure 3-4).

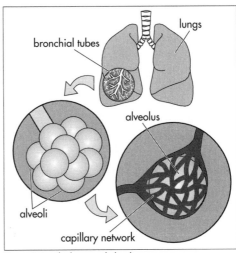

Figure 3-4 The lungs and alveoli.

Gas Exchange

The physical process of the lungs correlates with a biological process. When you inhale, the alveoli fill with air, and oxygen is then absorbed into the bloodstream through the network of capillaries which help to form the outer membrane of each alveolus. As the blood circulates through the body, the cells are fed this oxygen. The cells then give off the waste product carbon dioxide (Figure 3-5).

Carbon dioxide has a very important role in this continuous process: It tells the body when to breathe. It is a buildup of carbon dioxide rather than a lack of oxygen that stimulates the respiratory center of the brain and

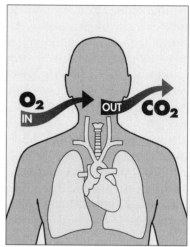

Figure 3-5 As the blood circulates through the body, the cells are fed oxygen. The cells then give off the waste product carbon dioxide.

creates the urge to inhale. The diaphragm and chest then relax, which makes you exhale. Carbon dioxide again builds up and this signals the body to inhale again, and so on.

Another gas that participates in this process is nitrogen. Although oxygen is the gas which sustains life, it only constitutes about 20% of the air you breathe, while about 80% is nitrogen. Nitrogen is actually an inert gas and is not used by the body.

This activity of the lungs and heart is rhythmic, keeping the exchange of gases consistent, even when responding to the varying needs of the body. Right now as you quietly read, your breathing and heart rate are relaxed. When you go for a run, your body's needs change and you have to breathe deeper and faster to get the required amount of oxygen. But even in this situation, your body's natural tendency is to breathe normally that is, to maintain a steady rhythm which keeps the exchange of gases balanced.

However, a steady rhythm can be interrupted; overexertion and excitement can cause you to breathe very fast and shallow. This shallow breathing can then lead to an adverse chain reaction (Figure 3-6):

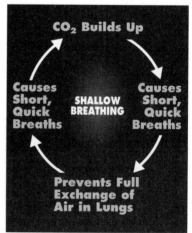

Figure 3-6 Shallow breathing can lead to an adverse chain reaction.

- Shallow breathing doesn't allow carbon dioxide to be vented off fully...
- This retained carbon dioxide buildup then signals the need to breathe sooner than normal...
- Short, quick breaths can then prevent the exchange of a large enough amount of air in the lungs...
- This causes the person to breathe harder to try to compensate for feeling out of breath...
- Which in turn causes anxiety, further complicating things.

Unless a diver stops, thinks, and gets breathing under control, stress, and even panic, may result.

Sustained shallow breathing and/or overexertion can cause an excess of carbon dioxide in the diver's body. Symptoms include labored breathing and shortness of breath. To prevent carbon dioxide excess, avoid overexertion. Any time breathlessness occurs, stop and rest until breathing is normal. The symptoms will disappear when the *cause* is eliminated.

Develop a pattern of inhaling steadily and slowly, then exhaling steadily. Inhalation and exhalation should be done one after the other without pause. Also remember **never to hold your breath**; even if the regulator is out of your mouth while under water, keep exhaling a steady stream of bubbles (Figure 3-7).

Figure 3-7   Remember never to hold your breath; even if the regulator is out of your mouth while under water, keep exhaling a steady stream of bubbles.

A poorly tuned or inadequate regulator can also lead to respiratory distress. It is important that you have a regulator designed for the type of diving that you will be doing and that you have it serviced regularly.

Don't make the mistake, however, of believing that breathing problems that may lead to stress *will* arise. Scuba diving is a safe and comfortable activity when correct procedures are followed—and one of these is simply to breathe normally and constantly.

Respiratory First Aid

If the gas exchange process ever completely breaks down, this is called *asphyxiation*, and when asphyxia occurs in water it can lead to drowning. If someone stops breathing it is very important to get breathing started again by means of *artificial respiration*, also known as *rescue breathing*.

Unless breathing is restored, the heart will also stop within a few minutes. When this happens, *cardiopulmonary resuscitation* (CPR) must be performed.

It is important to remember that while being prepared for *problems*, being a prepared *diver* will prevent problems from arising in the first place. There are a few precautions all divers should take. These may never become necessary but do add an extra measure of security to an already safe activity, and a valuable measure of competence to the diver.

■ *Take a CPR and Rescue Breathing Course.* Rescue breathing and CPR should only be performed by persons who are trained in the techniques. It is recommended that anyone involved in

National Safety Council

aquatic activities should be CPR trained. Courses may be offered through the National Safety Council (or through the International Safety Council outside of the US) by your SSI Dealer.

■ *Know Phone Numbers.* Know how to contact, from land and boat, the local ambulance, EMS system and/or dive rescue service for the region. Write all contact information in your divelog. Your country may also have a national medical information network for divers such as Divers Alert Network (DAN). Consult your SSI Instructor.

■ *Know Phone Location.* Locate the telephone nearest to where you are diving and make sure it's accessible.

■ *Recognize Stress.* Watch for erratic behavior in your buddy, and be aware of signs of stress in yourself. Obvious signs of stress under water are rapid, shallow breathing and a wide-eyed expression. If signs of stress are present, stop, breathe normally and think. If necessary, make a proper ascent to the surface with your buddy. The prevention of panic in a stressful situation by calm, corrective action is much easier and more effective than dealing with a panicked diver. SSI offers a course called *Diver Stress and Rescue* that shows divers how to deal with these problems.

■ *Alert Others, Get Help.* If a diver is injured or ill, alert other people in the area. Whether you are on land or in the water, call for help and get others to assist you in caring for the victim. You must assist the victim until professional medical help arrives.

■ *Get Victim Out of the Water.* If you are in the water, get the victim onto the shore or deck as soon as possible. Efforts to perform rescue breathing or first aid while in the water may interfere with the quickest possible removal of the victim from the water.

Lastly, while it is important to know emergency precautions, properly trained divers who use good judgement should never need to use them, or make it necessary for others to use them.

ADAPTING TO THE UNDERWATER ENVIRONMENT

Breathing under water will come easily and will soon become second nature. This will open the way to becoming more and more comfortable and able as a diver. You can begin to concentrate on your buoyancy, seeing and staying warm under water, and on learning how to communicate with your buddy and others while diving.

BUOYANCY

In diving, the body needs to be neutrally buoyant so that it isn't constantly fighting tendencies to either float up or sink down (Figure 3-8). Establishing neutral buoyancy is a matter of balancing many factors, the first of which is compensating for the diver's own personal tendency to either float or sink.

Figure 3-8   The body needs to be neutrally buoyant so that it isn't constantly fighting tendencies to either float up or sink down.

The individual's body will fall into one of three buoyancy categories: It will have *positive buoyancy*, or float; it will have *negative buoyancy*, or sink; or it will have *neutral buoyancy*, or will tend neither to float nor sink. Given the body's volume, if it weighs more than an equal volume of water, it will sink; if it is lighter than the same volume of water, it will float. This holds true of any object. The physical law which determines this is called **Archimedes' Principle**. This law states that **an object is buoyed up by a force equal to the weight of the water it displaces.**

Proper Weighting

A diver wearing an exposure suit and the equipment being used on the dive need to be positively buoyant when resting at the surface. At depth, the diver needs to be neutrally buoyant. Exposure suits typically add buoyancy to a diver's natural body buoyancy, so the first adjustment you need to make is weighting in order to establish neutral buoyancy at the surface with the BC deflated. Proper weighting is what allows the diver to get under water and begin a descent. With proper weighting achieved, adjustment of buoyancy under water is accomplished by adding air to or subtracting air from the BC.

To properly weight yourself you need to be wearing the weight system and all the other equipment you'll have on during the dive. Enter the water and first test that you are not greatly over-weighted. Then move to an area where you are suspended upright in water over your head. Your objective is to be able neither to float nor sink at the surface with the weight system on and the BC deflated. As you inhale, your eyes should rise slightly above the surface; as you exhale, you should sink below the surface, just enough to cover the top of your head. The water level should rise and fall around eye level. Add or remove weight as needed to achieve this (Figure 3-9).

Figure 3-9   As you inhale, your eyes should rise slightly above the surface; as you exhale, you should sink below the surface, just enough to cover the top of your head.

Controlling Buoyancy

When neutrally buoyant, you need to exhale to get below the surface and begin your descent feet-first. As divers descend, exposure suit buoyancy is reduced by compression, making the diver negatively buoyant. When your suit loses buoyancy and you begin to sink, add small amounts of air to the BC to compensate, so that you can control the descent (Figure 3-10).

When you want to stabilize at a depth, you can establish neutral buoyancy with a method similar

Figure 3-10   Add small amounts of air to the BC so that you can control the descent.

to the surface procedure. Instead
of adding or subtracting weight to
establish neutral buoyancy, you
add or subtract small amounts of
air to the BC until you become
suspended. When you are neutrally buoyant you will rise slightly
when you inhale and sink slightly
when you exhale (Figure 3-11).

Figure 3-11   When you are neutrally buoyant you
will rise slightly when you inhale and sink slightly when
you exhale.

If you feel unbalanced in the
water, leaning too far backward,
you may need to move your
weights slightly forward to counteract the weight of the tank. This
will allow you to more easily float
in an upright or forward position.

The BC also aids in ascending.
Before beginning your ascent,
make certain that you are neutrally buoyant, adding air to the BC
only if necessary. Then all you
need to do is start your ascent by
gently kicking. As you ascend, the
air in the BC and your exposure
suit will expand because of
decreasing pressure, making you
more and more buoyant as you
move upward toward the surface.
This makes ascents very easy, but

Figure 3-12   Release air from the BC as you come
up, or your ascent will become more rapid and you
may lose control.

you also need to release air from the BC as you come up, or your ascent
will become more rapid and you may lose control (Figure 3-12). This is
one of the most important reasons for maintaining good buoyancy control. By ascending too fast you can lose track of your buddy, collide with
an unseen obstruction, or worse, risk overexpansion injury or decompression sickness.

Being too negative can also lead to difficulty. Becoming mesmerized
by the beauty of your surroundings is one thing, but unless you have
established neutral buoyancy, the next time you look at your depth gauge
you may find that you've unintentionally descended another twenty or
thirty feet. Negative buoyancy can also make you constantly work to stay
off the bottom and thereby risk overexertion. Negatively buoyant divers
also wreak havoc to the substrate and may be injured by unintentionally
contacting marine life such as sea urchins.

Controlling your buoyancy at depth requires practice, and is a skill you will discover to be essential. Once you've experienced the wonderful feeling of weightless suspension under water, and the ease it provides you while diving, you'll naturally want to become skillful at maintaining neutral buoyancy.

VISION

Water refracts light differently than air, causing objects to appear out of focus when viewed under water with the naked eye. One of the beneficial effects of the mask is that it restores the natural medium of air to the area surrounding the eyes, allowing the eyes to focus. In addition, the mask lens, in combination with water and the space behind the lens, makes objects appear to be

Figure 3-13   The mask lens, in combination with water and the space behind the lens, makes objects appear to be 25% closer and 33% larger to the diver.

25% closer and 33% larger to the diver (Figure 3-13). This is because light is refracted in the mask before entering the eye and focusing on the retina.

In addition to water refracting light, it also absorbs light. This affects the colors you see under water because different colors of the spectrum are absorbed at different depths, depending on the wavelength of the color. Low frequency reds are absorbed first, while high frequency blues and grays travel farther. For this reason the deeper you go, the less distinct color you see and colors will appear muted. This is why shallow diving is usually more colorful than deep diving (Figure 3-14a & b). The

Figure 3-14a   The deeper you go, the less distinct color you see and colors will appear muted.

Figure 3-14b   Shallow diving is usually more colorful than deep diving.

use of an artificial light, of course, will restore color under water, and it is highly recommended that you use a light even during a day-time dive to "see" the real colors of the reef life.

Under water, vision is also affected by *turbid water*—water with suspended particles such as minerals and organic matter. These particles scatter and absorb light, impairing vision (Figure 3-15). To learn more about diving in turbid water, ask your SSI Dealer about a *Night/Limited Visibility Diving* Specialty Course.

Figure 3-15   Under water, vision is also affected by turbid water.

COMMUNICATION

Normal human communication involves hearing and speaking, but both of these actions are adversely affected by the medium of water. Hearing is affected because sound waves travel about four times faster in water than in air. This makes it difficult to know the direction from which sound is coming. On land, sound travels slowly enough to be heard first by the ear nearest to the source of the sound, and then by the other ear, indicating direction. In water, sound travels so fast that you usu-ally can't distinguish the direction of its source.

The problem with speaking is that just like vision, speaking is meant to be done in the medi-um of air. While the vocal folds

> In water, sound travels so fast that you usually can't distinguish the direction of its source.

vibrate and create sound just as on land, the expelled air which carries that sound, in effect, runs into a wall of water. Other sounds, however, are easy to understand as well as hear. You can easily hear a boat motor, for instance, from a long distance. A sound all divers need to know is the clanking of a dive knife against a scuba tank. This is the universal signal to get another diver's attention (Figure 3-16).

Though speaking under water is nearly impossible, it is still very important to communicate with your buddy and other divers. To "speak" to each other, divers may use a slate and marker which usually attach to the BC. The most common way divers communicate is by using a number of hand signals devised by the diving community (Figure 3-17, pages 100-101). Some divers use slight variations of these signals, so before you dive make sure you go over signals and agree upon the ones you will be using and what they mean (Figure 3-18). It is imperative that both of you know the emergency signals.

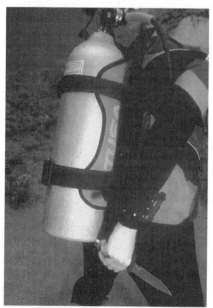

Figure 3-16   The clanking of a dive knife against a scuba tank is the universal signal to get another diver's attention.

Figure 3-18   Before you dive make sure you go over signals and agree upon the ones you will be using and what they mean.

EXPOSURE

Anyone who swims knows that when you first jump into water, even if it's relatively warm water, it feels cold. The reason for this is that the body operates at 98.6° F (37° C) and the water is usually much less than that. Further, the body loses heat faster in water than it does in air—twenty-five times faster. But it doesn't take long to "get used to it." What actually happens when you get used to the cold is that blood vessels in the skin are constricted, and less blood flows to the surface of the body. This slows down heat loss, and works to keep the body warm at its core where heat is more vital. But if the body remains exposed to the water for long, this reduced blood flow will not be enough to keep you warm and the body will try to generate heat by the muscle contractions called *shivering*. You need to terminate your dive well before this happens.

In very cold water this will happen sooner, and if the body is allowed to lose heat continually over a period of time, body temperature will actually begin to drop, shivering will become intense and prolonged, and extremities will begin to get numb. When body temperature is allowed to drop to 95°F (35°C), hypothermia sets in. If allowed to drop to 90°F (32°C), reasoning ability will begin to fail, and any temperature below 90°F (32°C) is life threatening. If you ever begin to shiver while diving, stop the dive, get out of the water and rewarm.

Use your exposure suit components to ensure temperature stability (refer to Chapter 2) and make optional decisions, such as whether or not to wear a hood and gloves, conservatively. For example, if you think you *might* need a hood, go ahead and wear it. It is easier for your body to cool down in a liquid medium than it is to rewarm once it has cooled. Remember, your comfort affects your enjoyment.

EFFECTS OF INCREASING PRESSURE

As already mentioned, breathing is something we are normally unaware of until we try to do it under unusual conditions, such as under water. Something else we're unaware of most of the time is that our bodies are constantly under pressure. Like breathing, this is something you will certainly become aware of as soon as you enter water.

We have all experienced the effects of increasing pressure when swimming (Figure 3-19). Many of us remember what it was like as a youngster to dive for coins at our local swimming pool, or to go down and touch the drain. There was always that moment of bravery in those last few feet when the pressure began to make your ears hurt. The reason for our discomfort was that pressure increases very fast as

Figure 3-19 We have all experienced the effects of increasing pressure when swimming.

you descend. As a diver you need to know how changes in pressure affect your body and how to compensate for them.

Figure 3-17   Hand signals.

13. Talk

14. Go back/ Back to starting point

15. Question?

16. Ship/ Boat

17. I am cold

18. This spot/ Right here

19. Cut

20. Which direction?

21. Hurry/ Faster

22. Distress/ Help (On surface)

23. Something overhead

24. Ok?/ Ok. (On surface at a distance)

25. Ok?/ Ok. (One hand occupied)

Ambient Pressure

Ambient pressure, or "surrounding pressure," as applied to diving, refers to the sum of air pressure and water pressure. At sea level, atmospheric pressure is about 14.7 psi (1 bar). That is the measure of the downward force of air in an imaginary one-inch (25 mm) square column from the top of the atmosphere to sea level, about 60 miles (100 km) (Figure 3-20).

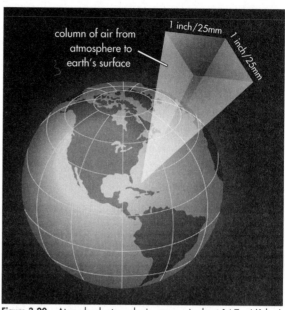

Figure 3-20 At sea level, atmospheric pressure is about 14.7 psi (1 bar).

The reason a diver experiences discomfort or pain in the ears at a depth as shallow as ten feet, as in the case of the youngster diving for coins, is that water is much more dense, and therefore heavier than air, and its pressure increases rapidly as you go deeper. In fact, it only takes a descent of 33 feet (10 metres) under water to experience the same amount of pressure as the atmospheric pressure caused by 60 miles (100 km) of air. It is said that at 33 feet (10 metres), there are two *atmospheres* of pressure (the weight of air plus the weight of water), or 29.4 psi (2 bar) of ambient pressure. This figure is achieved by multiplying 2 atmospheres X 14.7 psi to equal 29.4 psi (2 X 1 bar = 2 bar). And for every 33 feet (10 metres) deeper, another atmosphere of pressure is added due to the weight of additional water. So, at 66 feet (20 metres) or three atmospheres, there is 44.1 psi (3 X 14.7 psi = 44.1 psi) or 3 bar (3 X 1 bar = 3) of ambient pressure, and so forth (Figure 3-21).

Equalizing Pressure

Now, how does that pressure affect the diver? First, the human body is made up of approximately 70% water and about 30% solids and gases. Water and solids are not compressible. Where the difference lies for divers is within those areas of the body which contain gases. Included in this part of our makeup are air spaces: the sinuses, middle ears, and lungs.

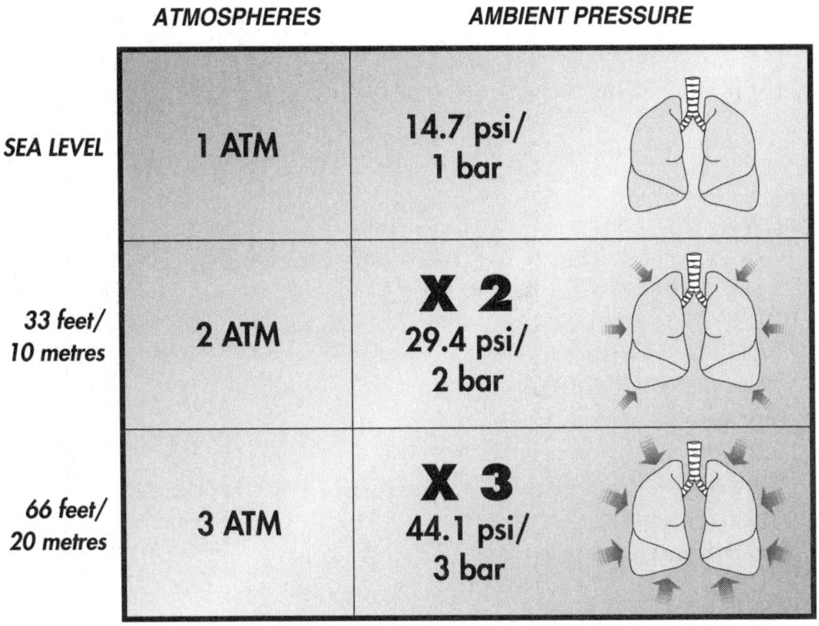

	ATMOSPHERES	AMBIENT PRESSURE	
SEA LEVEL	1 ATM	14.7 psi/ 1 bar	
33 feet/ 10 metres	2 ATM	**X 2** 29.4 psi/ 2 bar	
66 feet/ 20 metres	3 ATM	**X 3** 44.1 psi/ 3 bar	

Figure 3-21   Ambient pressure.

Unlike water and solids, gases *are* compressible. What this means for the diver who is descending is that unless somehow compensated for, increasing pressure will compress those air spaces of the body. At 33 feet (10 metres), where the body is under two atmospheres of pressure, the volume of the body's flexible air spaces would be reduced by one half. This phenomenon is described by **Boyle's Law**, which explains that **given a constant temperature, the volume of a gas decreases at the same rate surrounding pressure increases.**

As the volume of the gas compresses, the pressure of the gas remains equal to ambient, or outside, pressure. If the volume of that gas is enclosed in a flexible space, there is also a way to keep the pressure of the gas equal to ambient without allowing the volume to decrease and the space to shrink. By injecting a greater amount of gas into a given volume, the pressure of the gas remains equal to ambient pressure, but the volume of the space in which that gas is held stays the same. This is called *equalizing* (or the process of introducing higher pressure air which is being breathed by scuba into the air spaces) (Figure 3-22, next page). Without equalization the diver will experience a *squeeze*. That young diver who followed a coin to the bottom of the pool felt a minor *ear squeeze.*

There are air spaces within the diver's body and equipment which are subject to squeezes, and for each there is a method of equalizing.

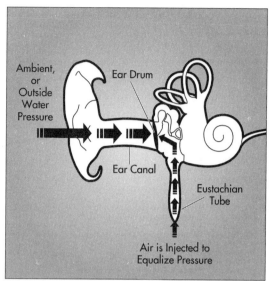

■ *Ears.* Under water the eardrum acts as a wall between water and air. An ear squeeze occurs when water pressure in the ear canal pushes harder against the outside of the eardrum than the air pressure pushing from the inside. To equalize ears, pinch the nose shut and blow gently (Figure 3-23). This will allow air pressure to pass from the lungs through the eustachian tubes into the middle ear. Sometimes it's easier to equalize ears by wiggling the jaw, swallowing, or yawning.

Figure 3-22 By injecting a greater amount of gas into a given volume, the pressure of the gas remains equal to ambient pressure, but the volume of the space in which that gas is held stays the same. This is called equalizing.

Ear equalization, or "clearing," should be started immediately upon descending and continued as you dive deeper, and should never be done forcefully. In fact,

Figure 3-23 To equalize ears, pinch the nose shut and blow gently.

you can test for equalization at the surface by **gently** clearing. Failure to clear ears can result in a serious injury. Rupture of the eardrum can result from unequalized ears, even in very shallow water. Damage can also occur when a diver tries to equalize too forcefully when the ears are blocked.

Symptoms of an ear injury can include ear pain, dizziness, nausea, and hearing difficulty. Victims of ear injury should seek medical attention.

■ **Sinuses.** The passageways into your sinus cavities are normally open. So, when you take a breath from your regulator, air flows from your mouth into your sinuses and equalizes the pressure. The same process of "equalizing" your middle ear areas will clear your sinuses.

Sinus equalization can be hampered by a blockage of the opening to the sinuses created by swelling or congestion due to colds, allergies, infection, or some other disorder. This can result in pain in the forehead, between the eyes, in the cheekbones, and sometimes in the upper teeth.

If your sinuses are blocked, it is best not to dive until the problem is resolved and they are open again.

■ **Equipment.** Of all your equipment, a squeeze will be felt most commonly in the *mask*. The space it encloses is large compared to the middle ear and sinuses, and unless that space is equalized you will feel the mask tighten against your face and eyes. To equalize the mask, gently exhale through the nose into the mask until it feels comfortable again (Figure 3-24).

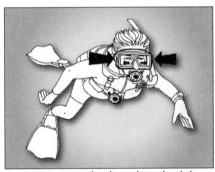

Figure 3-24 To equalize the mask, gently exhale through the nose into the mask.

Hoods can trap air in the ear canal. The trapped air may cause difficulty in equalizing the pressure in the ears. To help prevent this, divers can cut a small hole in the hood in the ear area, or you can pull the hood away from the head to let water into the hood. This lets in water so that the pressure can be equalized. If possible, exhaling air into the hood can also help.

■ **Lungs.** As a swimmer or a snorkeler, when you take a breath, hold it, and descend, the air in your lungs compresses and the volume of your lungs decreases, just as if you were exhaling. This is not dangerous because you would have to swim down to an extreme depth for this compression to become a problem.

When scuba diving, every time you take a breath from your regulator it delivers air at the same pressure as the surrounding water (ambient pressure). When you take a normal, full breath, your lungs are automatically equalized. There is nothing you need to do to equalize your lungs except breathe.

EFFECTS OF DECREASING PRESSURE

Whereas increasing pressure decreases the volume of gas, the opposite is also true: *decreasing* pressure allows gas to expand. This concept is easy to understand, but must also be understood in the context of diving, as gas expansion can be the cause of a serious diving injury. For instance, if you filled a balloon at 66 feet (20 metres) under 3 atmospheres of pressure and then began to ascend, the air inside would need to expand to three times the volume by the time it reached the surface (Figure 3-25). Would the balloon hold that volume of air?

The air spaces of your body are subject to the same thing. Your sinuses and ears will allow air to escape naturally, equalizing as you go, but the diver must consciously allow air to escape the lungs. It is extremely important for the diver to breathe normally while ascending. As long as you breathe normally, the airway will remain open. **Never hold your breath.** Breathing normally means that when you are not inhaling, you are exhaling, so you are breathing at all times. Even in the rare case of an emergency when getting to the surface is a priority, the diver *must* remember to breathe normally so that air can escape the lungs as diminishing outside pressure allows the air inside them to expand. Tilting the head back and looking up will also help keep the airway open.

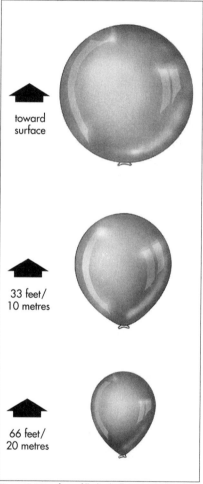

toward surface

33 feet/ 10 metres

66 feet/ 20 metres

Figure 3-25   If you filled a balloon at 66 feet (20 metres) under 3 atmospheres of pressure and then began to ascend, the air inside would need to expand to three times the volume by the time it reached the surface.

Overexpansion Injuries

Failure to keep an open airway to the lungs upon ascent can result in one of four overexpansion injuries. If a diver ascends without breathing normally and instead holds his or her breath, trapped gas in the lungs must find a way to escape. When lung tissue ruptures and air bubbles pass into the blood stream, the diver may experience an *air embolism* (Figure 3-26a, b, c, & d). The blood will carry these air bubbles into smaller arteries until a blockage forms and restricts blood flow. This can happen in various areas of the body, but some air bubbles in the bloodstream may travel to the brain. This can eventually cut off circulation to brain tissue, resulting in the most serious example of an embolism. Symptoms of air embolism can be as slight as numbness in an arm or leg, or a temporary loss of vision, hearing, or speech, or they can be as serious as paralysis and unconsciousness, and may even lead to death.

Air may also escape a damaged lung into the space between the heart, lungs and windpipe called the mediastinum. This is known as

Figure 3-26a Air embolism.

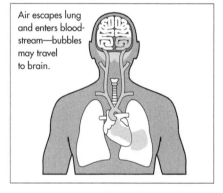

Air escapes lung and enters bloodstream—bubbles may travel to brain.

Figure 3-26b Mediastinal emphysema.

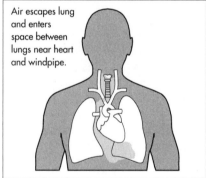

Air escapes lung and enters space between lungs near heart and windpipe.

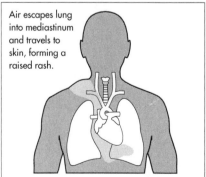

Air escapes lung into mediastinum and travels to skin, forming a raised rash.

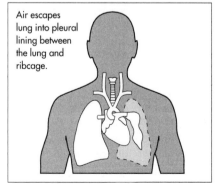

Air escapes lung into pleural lining between the lung and ribcage.

Figure 3-26c Subcutaneous emphysema.

Figure 3-26d Pneumothorax.

mediastinal emphysema. It results in air pressure against the heart and can cause chest pain, breathing difficulty, and faintness.

These bubbles in the mediastinum can also travel up along the windpipe and gather under the skin in the neck or upper chest, resulting in *subcutaneous emphysema*, a thick, raised rash which can impair speech and breathing if located near the larynx.

The lungs are separated from the chest wall by a membrane called the pleural lining. If air bubbles escape into the space between the lungs and the pleural lining, a pocket of air can form which in an extreme case can collapse the lung when that air expands and squeezes the lung as the diver ascends. This injury is called *pneumothorax.* It causes a shortness of breath and chest pain.

The current medical thinking describes both overexpansion injuries, including arterial gas embolism (AGE) and decompression sickness (DCS), as *decompression illness (DCI)* for purposes of treatment. Overexpansion injuries and DCS have such similar symptoms that they should all be treated as decompression illness until such a time as it is determined otherwise. The injured diver will need immediate medical care, therefore getting proper medical help is your first priority. If possible, the transportation of a victim to a medical facility is best handled by professionals. Any victim of DCI may require recompression in a *hyperbaric chamber*, or "recompression chamber" as it is sometimes called.

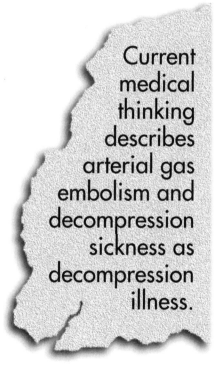

Current medical thinking describes arterial gas embolism and decompression sickness as decompression illness.

Before transport to a medical facility, or until professional medical attention is available, the victim must be stabilized (Figure 3-27):

- Remove the injured person from danger.
- Manage the ABC's of basic life support.
- Provide 100% oxygen.
- Activate the local emergency medical system (EMS) immediately. Know the phone numbers for the local EMS.

■ Contact the Divers Alert Network (DAN). They can make sure the injured person is being managed properly and will take care of the referral to the closest available recompression facility (This service is available to everyone, regardless of membership or insurance status with DAN.) **The DAN hotline is 919/684-8111.**

■ If the diver has serious symptoms and has breathed under water, CPR or rescue breathing with the highest possible concentration of oxygen may be necessary.

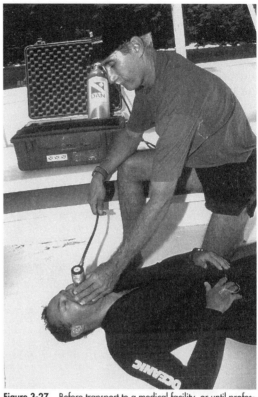

Figure 3-27 Before transport to a medical facility, or until professional medical attention is available, the victim must be stabilized.

Part of being a buddy is being responsive to your buddy's needs, in any situation. Being a good athlete or a comfortable diver, or even a helpful dive partner does not necessarily make you a good buddy. Being a buddy not only takes competence and caring, it takes responsibility. If you and your buddy are not familiar with basic first-aid and rescue techniques, it is a good idea to take an SSI/National Safety Council first-aid and CPR course. Find out about classes and seminars by contacting your local SSI Dealer. Plus, you can learn more about rescue procedures by taking an SSI *Diver Stress and Rescue* course.

It is a good idea to take an SSI/National Safety Council first-aid and CPR course.

ASCENT PROCEDURES

All it takes to avoid overexpansion problems is diving "healthy," breathing all the time and following correct ascent procedures. Get into the habit of using these procedures by performing them every time you ascend, regardless of depth.

NORMAL ASCENTS (Figure 3-28, facing page)

1. Check with your buddy, making sure you are both ready to ascend, then plan to ascend together (Figure 3-28a).

2. Place in view any instruments you are using to keep track of your rate of ascent. Go slow in any normal ascent (Figure 3-28b).

3. Hold the inflator hose upright in your left hand with the arm extended and vent air from the BC if necessary to control your ascent. This will also keep one arm positioned above to warn you of possible obstructions overhead (Figure 3-28c).

4. Facing your buddy, look toward the surface and select a clear path.

5. While neutrally buoyant, start your ascent by kicking gently upward. Periodically look upward to see what's above you and to check on your buddy's position.

6. Ascend at the rate of 30 feet (9 metres) per minute or less. You can keep track of your rate of ascent by monitoring your instruments.

7. Make a safety stop at 15 feet for 3-5 minutes (5 metres for 5 minutes) (Figure 3-28d).

8. Breathe normally and continuously all the way to the surface. Again, *never hold your breath*. Also, do not remove the regulator mouthpiece until after you have surfaced and inflated your BC.

9. When you reach the surface inflate the BC, do a weight system check (rehearsing what you would do if you needed to ditch the system), keep your mask in place, and either keep the regulator in place or switch to snorkel breathing.

AIR SHARING

Though it is unlikely you will ever run out of air, you must nevertheless be prepared for regulator malfunction or the possibility of an out-of-air situation because of low tank pressure at depth. When talking about

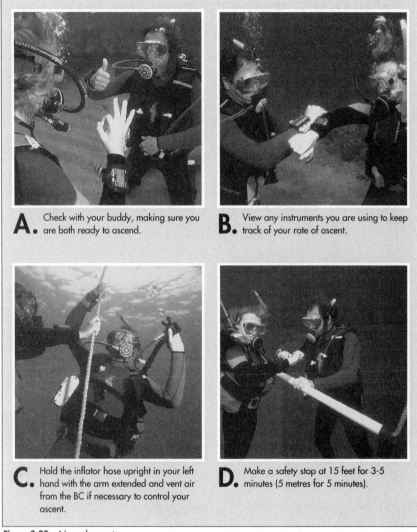

A. Check with your buddy, making sure you are both ready to ascend.

B. View any instruments you are using to keep track of your rate of ascent.

C. Hold the inflator hose upright in your left hand with the arm extended and vent air from the BC if necessary to control your ascent.

D. Make a safety stop at 15 feet for 3-5 minutes (5 metres for 5 minutes).

Figure 3-28   Normal ascents.

air sharing we refer to the buddy who needs air as the *needer* and the buddy who assists as the *donor*.

In a real life out-of-air situation there would be little opportunity to stop, think and act, but if you learn and rehearse the skills, you are more likely to use them when they are needed. A precaution all divers should take to be prepared for the possibility of running out of air is to *overlearn* air sharing and air sharing ascent procedures.

If a diver is having an air supply problem and a buddy is nearby, the needer would give the buddy, the donor, the hand signals for "out of air" and "let's share air." At that time the buddy would react in one of several ways depending on the exact circumstances (Figure 3-29). The primary concerns would be to get the needer breathing, and then get to the surface.

Figure 3-29   If a diver is having an air supply problem and a buddy is nearby, the needer would give the buddy, the donor, the hand signals for "out of air" and "let's share air."

ALTERNATE AIR SHARING ASCENTS

After being alerted by the needer, the donor should take control of the situation, offering the most immediately available air source. If the donor is equipped with an alternate air source such as an *inflator-integrated air source*, he or she would offer the primary second-stage to the needer, then locate the alternate air source to breathe from (Figure 3-30a). If the donor is equipped with a *double second-stage or octopus regulator*, the donor has the option to pass either the primary or the alternate regulator (Figure 3-30b). If either the donor or the needer is equipped

Figure 3-30a   With an inflator-integrated air source, the donor offers the primary second-stage to the needer, then locates the alternate air source to breathe from.

Figure 3-30b   With a double second-stage or octopus regulator, the donor can pass either the primary or the alternate regulator.

Figure 3-30c   If the donor or needer has an independent air source, the needer can breathe from it while the donor breathes from the primary regulator.

with an *independent air source*, the needer can breathe from it while the donor breathes from the primary regulator (Figure 3-30c). This is why you should always know the placement and type of alternate air source your buddy is using. Always do a pre-dive check for the alternate air source location and discuss the sharing air procedure.

After breathing is under control, the donor and needer have to establish a physical link (Figure 3-31). This can be accomplished by hooking the right arms together and holding onto each other's BCs or BC shoulder straps, keeping the

Figure 3-31   After breathing is under control, the donor and needer have to establish a physical link.

left arms of both divers free to control the inflators while ascending. After the donor determines that they're both ready, the divers should make a controlled ascent together (Figure 3-32).

Now, all this information about air sharing and being out of air under water can make you uneasy if taken in the wrong context. These are contingency skills. An air sharing situation will rarely, if ever, arise in recreational diving. But by knowing the skills, you add an extra element of certainty to your ability as a diver.

Figure 3-32   After the donor determines that they're both ready, the divers should make a controlled ascent together.

EMERGENCY ASCENTS

We've already discussed what to do in an air emergency when a buddy is ready to assist. But what if you have a problem with your air supply, are low on air, or out of air, and no one is there to help? Your only option would be to get to the surface quickly. There are two methods for ascending in an emergency: the *emergency swimming ascent* and the *emergency buoyant ascent*. First and foremost when talking about emergency ascents is the importance of maintaining proper buoyancy. Any time a diver needs to get to the surface quickly, an ascent is easiest to initiate when the diver is already at least neutral or slightly positive. It is very important to get into the habit of maintaining neutral buoyancy at all times while diving.

Emergency Swimming Ascent

If the diver becomes aware of being *low* on air, or has some other air supply problem which has not entirely shut off the air, he or she will be able to swim to the surface. *An emergency swimming ascent* is essentially the same as a normal ascent except that you are prepared to ditch your weight system for immediate positive buoyancy if necessary.

To make an emergency swimming ascent, hold your weight system release with the right hand, kick toward the surface, and vent air from the BC to control your ascent. Try to maintain a slow ascent rate. The reason for being poised to ditch the weights is that in many diving accidents the diver successfully reaches the surface, only to sink back down into the water (Figure 3-33). Fatalities have occurred because of this. This leads us to the main objective of the emergency buoyant ascent.

Emergency Buoyant Ascent

The *emergency buoyant ascent* is done in the case of a sudden loss of air which requires an immediate return to the surface. To perform the

> An emergency swimming ascent is essentially the same as a normal ascent except that you are prepared to ditch your weight system for immediate positive buoyancy if necessary.

Figure 3-33 The reason for being poised to ditch the weights is that in many diving accidents the diver successfully reaches the surface, only to sink back down into the water.

emergency buoyant ascent, the diver immediately ditches the weight system at depth, utilizing the *quick draw* method mentioned in Chapter 2. This provides positive buoyancy which begins lifting the diver. From depths beyond which the wet suit has lost its buoyancy, a gentle kick will assist the ascent.

While making the ascent, it is vital that the diver allow air to vent from the lungs by continuously exhaling. Also, just as with normal ascents, the diver should: 1) stay relaxed, 2) keep the head back, 3) look up, 4) hold the inflator hose aloft in the left hand, and 5) let air escape the BC during the ascent if necessary. To slow the ascent when approaching the surface, and to reduce the risk of injury, the diver can *flare* the body in the last twenty feet (six metres) or so. To flare, as you approach the surface lay back in the water and spread your arms and legs (Figure 3-34).

To perform the emergency buoyant ascent, the diver immediately ditches the weight system at depth.

The advantage of the buoyant ascent is that it assures the diver of surfacing, and the knowledge of this fact may even lessen the diver's

Figure 3-34   To reduce the risk of injury, the diver can flare the body in the last twenty feet (six metres) or so.

worries. If you are confused or panicked and there is a doubt about which ascent to use, ditch the weights and do the buoyant ascent. This covers all your bases: 1) you will surface, and 2) you'll stay there.

Only opt for surfacing if there is no way to solve a problem under water. With any ascent, only surface faster than 30 feet (9 metres) per minute when absolutely necessary; remember that you're risking overexpansion and/or decompression problems by ascending faster than 30 feet (9 metres) per minute.

If you do an emergency ascent, keep your regulator in your mouth all the way to the surface and attempt to inhale and exhale normally—do not hold your breath. Due to a number of factors such as low tank pressure, depth, and regulator performance, you may get some air from the scuba system as you ascend due to decreasing ambient pressure; additionally, any attempt to inhale will open the throat, which will help prevent overexpansion. If your regulator for some reason is out of your mouth, exhale all the way to the surface, but do not force the exhale. As long as the airway is open, air will flow out naturally.

> You may get some air from the scuba system as you ascend due to decreasing ambient pressure.

It is recommended that you always locate the weight system and mentally rehearse ditching it after you surface, every time you dive. Unlike normal diving skills, emergency skills need to be learned despite the fact that you may never use them. You need to learn these skills not just by reading about them, but by mentally rehearsing them every time you dive so that they will be second nature in case you ever *do* need them. An annual skills update is also highly recommended. See your SSI Dealer about taking a *Scuba Skills Update* course. It is a good idea to do this before each diving season as a refresher course.

SUMMARY

This chapter is full of technical information, possible hazards, and emergency and first aid advice. Don't let it overwhelm you or lead you to believe that you've gotten yourself in over your head, so to speak. It still holds that diving is easy and fun when a properly trained and equipped diver performs the skills properly. There's no mystery, just knowledge and practice. Diving injuries and fatalities usually happen because of lack of training, poor judgement, divers exceeding personal limits of skill level or physical capacity, or panic. Seldom do accidents occur due to equipment failure or environmental conditions. Basic knowledge of your physiology and the physics of diving will help you develop proper behaviors and an informed attitude that will keep you and your buddy out of trouble under water.

Depth, Time, and the Diver

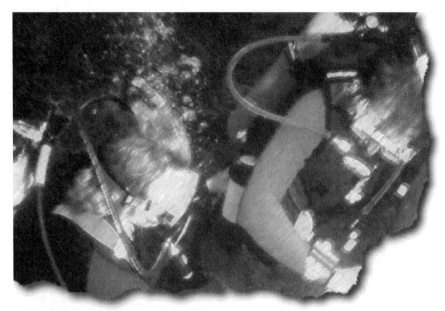

Chapter 4:
Depth, Time, and the Diver

Some effects of pressure will be felt immediately in the diver's body. Minor pressure on the ears and inside the mask will alert the diver of the need to avoid problems by equalizing. There are, however, other effects of pressure on the body that are not so easily felt, but must also be recognized and compensated for. These effects have to do with diving for a certain period of time at a specific depth, and with diving too deep.

This brings us to the importance of dive planning. Everyone has heard stories about "the bends" when a diver suddenly experiences a paralysis in a muscle or joint, or reports of mental confusion when a diver can no longer tell the difference between a depth gauge and a wristwatch due to the narcotic effects of too much nitrogen in the blood. By planning a safe dive and sticking to the plan, problems having to do with nitrogen, such as decompression sickness, can certainly be minimized. Just as with over-expansion problems, it takes knowledge of the physical phenomena your body is subject to, and familiarization with some scuba skills in order to enjoy the beautiful underwater world.

EFFECTS OF BREATHING COMPRESSED AIR: PARTIAL PRESSURES

BREATHING AT THE SURFACE

Air is a mixture of gases, about 20% oxygen and 80% nitrogen. At sea level we breathe air at 14.7 psi or 1 bar of pressure. Since 20% of the total is oxygen, the pressure of oxygen in air at sea level is 2.94 psi or .2 bar (20% of 14.7 psi or 1 bar). The pressure of nitrogen at sea level is then 11.76 psi or .8 bar (80% of 14.7 psi/1 bar). This is expressed in a simple law of physics called *Dalton's Law,* which explains that the pressure of a gas mixture is made up of the sum of the *partial pressures* of the gases in that mixture (Figure 4-1).

After we take oxygen and nitrogen into the lungs, the gases move through our bodies serving different purposes: the oxygen is our body's fuel.

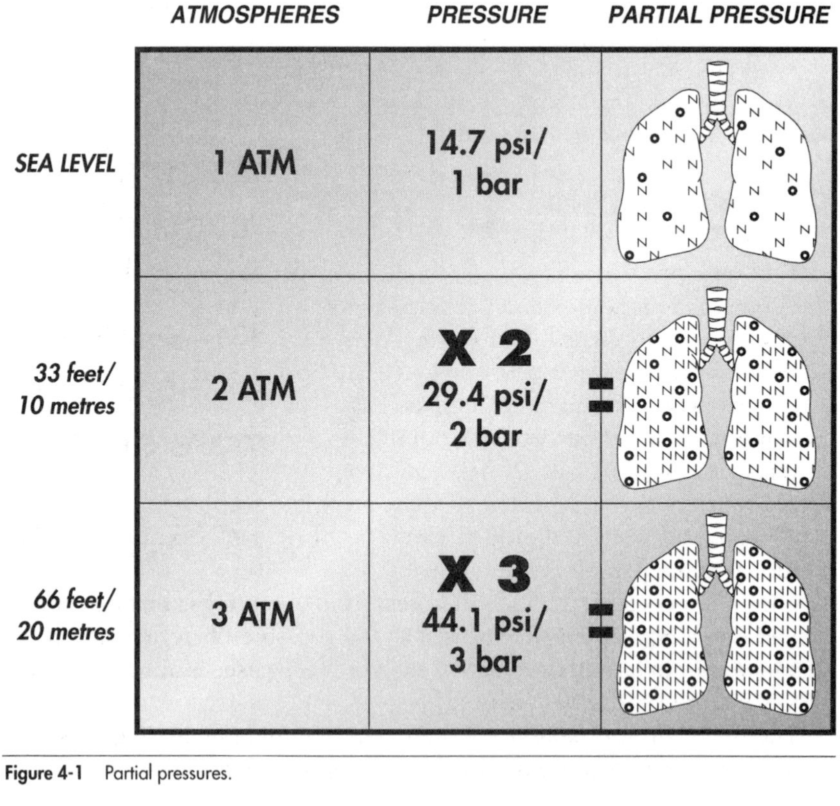

	ATMOSPHERES	PRESSURE	PARTIAL PRESSURE
SEA LEVEL	1 ATM	14.7 psi/ 1 bar	
33 feet/ 10 metres	2 ATM	**X 2** 29.4 psi/ 2 bar	
66 feet/ 20 metres	3 ATM	**X 3** 44.1 psi/ 3 bar	

Figure 4-1   Partial pressures.

Oxygen is needed by our bodies to sustain life. The blood in our circulatory system picks up the oxygen and carries it to our tissues. At the tissue level, the oxygen is used and in the process produces carbon dioxide, which is then carried by the blood back to the lungs and exhaled.

Nitrogen, however, is not needed by the body and is not used or processed. Now, just like oxygen, it is a gas, and gases can be dissolved into liquids. Our blood absorbs nitrogen from the lungs and carries it in liquid solution out to our tissues. Once delivered, it simply stays there as nitrogen in solution; it is not used, as is oxygen.

Assuming that we have been breathing air at sea level for some time, our bodies are *saturated* with nitrogen at sea level pressure. So, all throughout our tissues nitrogen is in solution at 11.76 psi (.8 bar). As long as we stay at sea level, this concentration of nitrogen will not increase or decrease, thus posing no threat to us.

BREATHING AIR UNDER WATER

When we breathe under water, the regulator delivers air to our lungs at the same pressure as surrounding water (ambient pressure). So, when we take a breath at 33 feet (10 metres), for example, the total pressure in our lungs is 29.4 psi (2 bar), or two times sea level pressure.

At depth, the volume of air in our lungs is the same, but the gas is more dense. Essentially, we breathe more molecules of the gases as we go deeper, and the partial pressure of each gas increases in proportion to the total surrounding pressure. As we continue to descend, the total ambient pressure increases, and so do the partial pressures of oxygen and nitrogen.

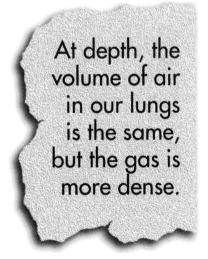

At depth, the volume of air in our lungs is the same, but the gas is more dense.

Under these conditions of increasing pressures another simple law of physics comes into play. *Henry's Law* explains that the amount of a gas which dissolves into a liquid is proportional to the partial pressure of that gas. In other words, the higher the pressure, the more gas that can be dissolved into a liquid. This means that as the pressure of oxygen and nitrogen increases in the lungs, more of each of these gases is absorbed by the blood and then carried to the tissues.

The two main problems associated with breathing increasing pressures of nitrogen are *nitrogen narcosis* and *decompression sickness*.

NITROGEN NARCOSIS

High pressure nitrogen has a narcotic effect on humans. It can cause an abnormal sense of euphoria and well-being, nervous symptoms, and a slowing down or dulling of the normal functions of the brain. It is not known exactly why nitrogen has this effect, although many scientists liken it to the effect of anesthesia.

Symptoms can be very mild at first and increase as the diver goes deeper. When affected by high pressure nitrogen, a diver may have difficulty doing things that would normally be easy, such as reading and interpreting instruments, making decisions, operating a BC correctly, or communicating with a buddy. Nitrogen narcosis can cause dizziness or disorientation, and if the diver continues to descend, eventually unconsciousness.

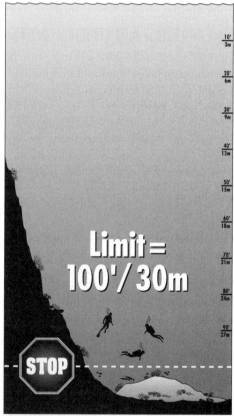

There is no time element involved in the onset of narcosis, or with relief from it. Symptoms can occur immediately upon arrival at a depth, and will be relieved as soon as the diver moves to a shallower depth—there is no recovery period to speak of. This makes the cure easy: just ascend slowly to a shallower depth.

The depth at which symptoms occur cannot be precisely determined. Many divers will not report any recognizable symptoms of narcosis on dives shallower than 60 to 80 feet (18 to 24 metres). In the 80 to 100 feet (24 to 30 metre) range some divers will be noticeably affected.

Nitrogen narcosis is one of the main reasons it is recommended that recreational divers stay above 100 feet or 30 metres (Figure 4-2). However, with proper training and preparation, deeper dives can be made. See your instructor

Figure 4-2   Nitrogen narcosis is one of the main reasons it is recommended that recreational divers stay above 100 feet or 30 metres.

or SSI Dealer about specialized training in deep diving.

DECOMPRESSION SICKNESS

The possibility of decompression sickness is another problem associated with the increased partial pressure of nitrogen to which a diver is exposed when breathing under water.

As the diver descends and the partial pressure of nitrogen breathed into the lungs increases, the blood absorbs this extra nitrogen quite readily and carries it in solution out to the tissues. The tissues then absorb the nitrogen and keep it in solution under pressure.

When the diver moves back into shallower water and the partial pressure of nitrogen drops, the process is reversed. The blood coming from the lungs now has less nitrogen pressure, allowing the tissues to release nitrogen back into the blood, which then carries it back to the lungs where it is exhaled. During this process of releasing nitrogen from the tissues, it is important that the diver comes up slowly enough to allow the nitrogen to *stay in solution* in the tissues and blood while it is being released.

If the diver ascends too quickly, the nitrogen comes out of solution and forms gas bubbles in the tissues and blood which can cause blockages and create symptoms of decompression sickness. The simplest explanation of what causes decompression sickness is that nitrogen bubbles form in the body when a diver ascends too fast after breathing compressed air under water for a period of time.

The principle of bubble formation can be demonstrated by a bottle of carbonated beverage with a twist top. When the cap is on, the liquid is clear. There is no indication that the liquid contains a gas because the gas is in solution under pressure (4-3a). When you twist the cap off, bubbles immediately form in the liquid because of lessening pressure (Figure 4-3b).

Figure 4-3a The gas is in solution under pressure.

Figure 4-3b Bubbles immediately form in the liquid because of lessening pressure.

Symptoms

Depending on where the nitrogen bubble blockages form, a variety of problems can result (Figure 4-4). If the bubbles occur in the capillaries near the surface of the skin, an irritable rash may break out. Breathing difficulty, coughing, and a burning sensation in the chest signal a hit in a lung. If the blockage forms in a joint or muscle, pain will be felt in that area. A more serious hit in the spinal cord will result in loss of feeling and paralysis. And

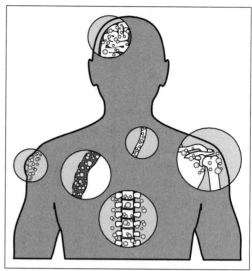

Figure 4-4 Depending on where the nitrogen bubble blockages form, a variety of problems can result.

just as with overexpansion injuries, the worst form of decompression sickness involves a hit in the brain, which can cause dizziness, paralysis, temporary blindness, convulsions, and unconsciousness. Symptoms usually appear within 15 minutes to 12 hours after surfacing, but can appear sooner. Delayed occurrence of symptoms is rare but can happen, especially if air travel or driving to altitude follows the dive.

First aid for the decompression illness victim includes 100% oxygen, or the highest concentration available.

First Aid and Treatment

As we discussed in Chapter 3, all compressed gas injuries, whether decompression sickness or arterial gas embolism, are treated as decompression illness. First aid for the decompression illness victim includes breathing as high a concentration of oxygen as is available, 100% if possible. Keeping the victim still, placing him or her in a comfortable position, and if conscious, giving nonalcoholic fluids such as water. See Chapter 3 for more information on first aid for decompression illness.

Treatment for decompression sickness is immediate recompression in a hyperbaric chamber (Figure 4-5). This reduces the size of the bubbles so that they can go back into solution. The diver is then brought out of pressure slowly enough to allow the nitrogen to be released as it should have been in the first place.

Again, as a precaution, all divers should know how to activate the emergency medical services for the region.

Figure 4-5 Treatment for decompression sickness is immediate recompression in a hyperbaric chamber.

Prevention

When diving, the two factors which determine how much nitrogen you absorb are depth and time. The deeper you go, the denser the air you breathe and the more nitrogen there is to absorb. The longer you stay under water, the more time your body has to accumulate nitrogen. The absorption of nitrogen by the tissues takes time, and it does not occur at the same rate throughout the body. Some tissues absorb and give off nitrogen very readily while others do so more slowly.

When you return to the surface, you don't need to bring the nitrogen level back to the same 11.76 psi (.8 bar) it was at the beginning of the dive. Your tissues can tolerate a certain amount of *supersaturation*—a higher concentration of nitrogen than would be absorbed at sea level. After a dive, while you are on the surface, you will continue to release nitrogen until you are back to that normal partial pressure at sea level. If you dive again before your nitrogen returns to this level, you have to take your present level into consideration, and so on throughout the day. This will become more clear when you learn how to use the dive tables in the next section of this chapter.

The key thing to remember about preventing decompression sickness is returning to the surface slowly enough to allow nitrogen to be released from the blood and tissues without coming out of solution. **The rate of ascent is 30 feet or 9 metres per minute.** During this slow ascent your body naturally vents off extra nitrogen (Figure 4-6).

Figure 4-6   During slow ascent your body naturally vents off extra nitrogen.

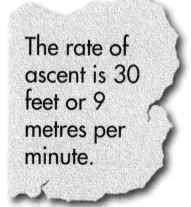

The rate of ascent is 30 feet or 9 metres per minute.

If divers surpass recommended time limits at certain depths, they are said to have made a *decompression dive* and therefore must make a *decompression stop* before surfacing. A decompression stop is required when a diver has taken on too much nitrogen to vent off during a normal ascent to the surface. Decompression diving is outside the scope of recreational scuba diving and increases the risk of decompression sickness.

Depth and time limits for no-decompression dives are on a chart devised by the U.S. Navy called the **U.S. Navy Dive Tables**. These tables show divers how to minimize the possibility of decompression sickness. Always stay within the Doppler depth and no-decompression time limits of the dive tables. Also, as an extra safety measure, always make a safety stop of 3-5 minutes at 15 feet on any dive over 30 feet or 9 metres. The recommended safety stop comes out of the 1989 *Biomechanics of Safe Ascents Workshop* which was sponsored by the American Academy of Underwater Sciences. Other countries, such as Japan and Australia, that recommend a 5-minute stop at 5 metres, have based this recommendation on studies from their own countries.

THE DIVE TABLES

The U.S. Navy developed several dive tables designed to minimize decompression problems by showing divers how to make dives that do not require decompression stops. The **U.S. Navy Dive Tables** cross-reference the number of *minutes* you can stay at certain *depths* without absorbing excess nitrogen into your body, and therefore have to make a required decompression stop before surfacing. They also tell divers how long to stay out of the water before making a subsequent dive.

The U.S. Navy Dive Tables were designed to Navy specifications for use by Navy divers. Sport divers use a slightly altered version of the tables. *Doppler ultrasound research* resulted in the *Doppler Line*, a more conservative combination of depths and times for no-decompression diving. Recreational divers should never make dives requiring decompression stops, and should also never "push" the limits. It is therefore recommended that you always stay within Doppler No-Decompression Limits (Figure 4-7).

Of course, there is no guarantee that staying even within these limits will insure safety. Every diver is different, and individual nitrogen absorption rates will vary to some degree. Dehydration, aerobic exercise and elevated body core temperature from hot tubs are examples which can add risk. Smart divers plan their dives well, and part of this planning is using the Doppler limits and staying conservatively within them. Monitoring your ascent rate, and the inclusion of a 3- to 5-minute stop at 15 feet or 5 metres adds a margin of safety.

Recreational divers should never push the limits of the dive tables.

DOPPLER NO-DECOMPRESSION LIMITS BASED ON U.S. NAVY DIVE TABLES

SCUBA SCHOOLS INTERNATIONAL **SSI**®

TABLE 1 — No-Decompression Limits and Repetitive Group Designation Table For No-Decompression Air Dives

HOW TO USE TABLE 1: Find the planned depth of your dive in feet or metres at the far left of Table 1. Read to the right until you find the time (minutes) you plan to spend at that depth. Read down to find the Group Designation letter.

DEPTH feet / metres		Doppler No-Decompression Limits (minutes)											
10	3.0		60	120	210	300							
15	4.5		35	70	110	160	225	350					
20	6.0		25	50	75	100	135	180	240	325			
25	7.5	245	20	35	55	75	100	125	160	195	245		
30	9.0	205	15	30	45	60	75	95	120	145	170	205	
35	10.5	160	5	15	25	40	50	60	80	100	120	140	160
40	12.0	130	5	15	25	30	40	50	70	80	100	110	130
50	15.0	70		10	15	25	30	40	50	60	70		
60	18.0	50		10	15	20	25	30	40	50			
70	21.0	40		5	10	15	20	30	35	40			
80	24.0	30		5	10	15	20	25	30				
90	27.0	25		5	10	12	15	20	25				
100	30.0	20		5	7	10	15	20					
110	33.0	15			5	10	13	15					
120	36.0	10			5	10							
130	39.0	5			5								

GROUP DESIGNATION: A B C D E F G H I J K

HOW TO USE TABLE 2:

Enter with the Group Designation letter from Table 1. Follow the arrow down to the corresponding letter on Table 2. To the left of these letters are windows of time. Read to the left until you find the times between which your surface interval falls. Then read down until you find your New Group Designation letter. Dives following surface intervals of more than 12 hours are not repetitive dives.

TABLE 2 — Residual Nitrogen Timetable For Repetitive Air Dives

REPETITIVE GROUP AT THE BEGINNING OF THE SURFACE INTERVAL

0:10 12:00*	**A**									
3:21 12:00*	0:10 3:20	**B**								
4:50 12:00*	1:40 4:49	0:10 1:39	**C**							
5:49 12:00*	2:39 5:48	1:10 2:38	0:10 1:09	**D**						
6:35 12:00*	3:25 6:34	1:58 3:24	0:55 1:57	0:10 0:54	**E**					
7:06 12:00*	3:58 7:05	2:29 3:57	1:30 2:28	0:46 1:29	0:10 0:45	**F**				
7:36 12:00*	4:26 7:35	2:59 4:25	2:00 2:58	1:16 1:59	0:41 1:15	0:10 0:40	**G**			
8:00 12:00*	4:50 7:59	3:21 4:49	2:24 3:20	1:42 2:23	1:07 1:41	0:37 1:06	0:10 0:36	**H**		
8:22 12:00*	5:13 8:21	3:44 5:12	2:45 3:43	2:03 2:44	1:30 2:02	1:00 1:29	0:34 0:59	0:10 0:33	**I**	
8:51 12:00*	5:41 8:50	4:03 5:40	3:05 4:02	2:21 3:04	1:48 2:20	1:20 1:47	0:55 1:19	0:32 0:54	0:10 0:31	**J**
8:59 12:00*	5:49 8:58	4:20 5:48	3:22 4:19	2:39 3:21	2:04 2:38	1:36 2:03	1:12 1:35	0:50 1:11	0:29 0:49	0:10 0:28	**K**

NEW GROUP DESIGNATION ▶	A	B	C	D	E	F	G	H	I	J	K

REPETITIVE DIVE DEPTH ▼   ▼RESIDUAL NITROGEN TIMES DISPLAYED ON REVERSE▼

Reorder Nº 2206

Figure 4-7 Dive Tables within Doppler No-Decompression Limits.

DOPPLER NO-DECOMPRESSION LIMITS BASED ON U.S. NAVY DIVE TABLES

SCUBA SCHOOLS INTERNATIONAL **SSI**®

TABLE 3 Residual Nitrogen Times (Minutes)

— CONTINUED FROM REVERSE SIDE —

NEW GROUP DESIGNATION ▶

= ADJUSTED NO-DECOMPRESSION TIME LIMITS   N/L=NO LIMIT

REPETITIVE DIVE DEPTH feet	metres	A	B	C	D	E	F	G	H	I	J	K
10	3	39 / N/L	88 / N/L	159 / N/L	279 / N/L							
20	6	18 / N/L	39 / N/L	62 / N/L	88 / N/L	120 / N/L	159 / N/L	208 / N/L	279 / N/L	399 / N/L		
30	9	12 / 193	25 / 180	39 / 166	54 / 151	70 / 135	88 / 117	109 / 96	132 / 73	159 / 46	190 / 15	
40	12	7 / 123	17 / 113	25 / 105	37 / 93	49 / 81	61 / 69	73 / 57	87 / 43	101 / 29	116 / 14	
50	15	6 / 64	13 / 57	21 / 49	29 / 41	38 / 32	47 / 23	56 / 14	66 / 4			
60	18	5 / 45	11 / 39	17 / 33	24 / 26	30 / 20	36 / 14	44 / 6				
70	21	4 / 36	9 / 31	15 / 25	20 / 20	26 / 14	31 / 9	37 / 3				
80	24	4 / 26	8 / 22	13 / 17	18 / 12	23 / 7	28 / 2					
90	27	3 / 22	7 / 18	11 / 14	16 / 9	20 / 5	24 / 1					
100	30	3 / 17	7 / 13	10 / 10	14 / 6	18 / 2						
110	33	3 / 12	6 / 9	10 / 5	13 / 2							
120	36	3 / 7	6 / 4	9 / 1								
130	39	3 / 2										

HOW TO USE TABLE 3:
Enter with the New Group Designation letter from Table 2. Next, find the planned depth of your repetitive dive in feet or metres at the far left of Table 3. The box that intersects the Repetitive Dive Depth and the New Group Designation will have two numbers. The top number indicates the Residual Nitrogen Time. The bottom number indicates the maximum Adjusted No-Decompression Time Limit for the next dive.

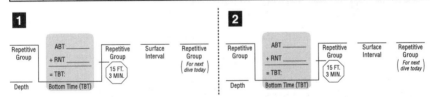

1

Repetitive Group	ABT _____
	+ RNT _____
	= TBT:
Depth	Bottom Time (TBT)

→ Repetitive Group (15 FT. 3 MIN.) → Surface Interval → Repetitive Group (For next dive today)

2

Repetitive Group	ABT _____
	+ RNT _____
	= TBT:
Depth	Bottom Time (TBT)

→ Repetitive Group (15 FT. 3 MIN.) → Surface Interval → Repetitive Group (For next dive today)

WARNING: *The U.S. Navy Dive Tables were designed to Navy specifications for use by Navy Divers. When used by recreational divers, the tables should be used conservatively. Even when used correctly with proper safety procedures,* ***decompression sickness may still occur.***

SAFETY STOP PROCEDURE: *It is recommended that you make a 3- to 5-minute safety stop at 15 feet (5 metres) on all dives over 30 feet (9 metres).*

OMITTED DECOMPRESSION PROCEDURE: *Should you exceed the Doppler No-Decompression Time Limits by less than 5 minutes on any dive, it is recommended that you ascend normally to 15 feet (5 metres) and stop for at least 10 minutes or longer if your air supply allows. Should you exceed the Doppler No-Decompression Time Limits by more than 5 minutes but less than 10 minutes on any dive, it is recommended that you stop at 15 feet (5 metres) for at least 20 minutes or longer if your air supply allows.*

Refrain from any further scuba diving activities for at least 24 hours.

Reorder Nº 2206

DIVE TABLE TERMINOLOGY

Before we begin to explain the dive tables, we must all speak the same language, or use the same terminology. Listed below are some of the key terms you must know in order to help you better understand how to use the dive tables.

- **No-Decompression Dive.** Any dive that can be made to a certain depth for a maximum amount of time so that a direct ascent can be made to surface; a dive that does not require decompression stops in order to reduce excess nitrogen.

- **Doppler Limits.** More conservative recommended no-decompression time limits at depth than the U.S. Navy time limits, based on Doppler Ultrasound Research.

- **Repetitive Dive.** Any dive started between 10 minutes and 12 hours after a previous scuba dive.

- **Group Designation Letter.** The letter assigned after a dive which indicates the amount of residual nitrogen remaining in the diver's tissues.

- **Surface Interval.** The amount of time the diver stays out of the water or on the surface between dives, beginning as soon as the diver surfaces and ending at the start of the next descent.

- **Decompression Dive.** A dive that exceeds the no-decompression time limits of the U.S. Navy Dive Tables, thus requiring planned decompression stops to eliminate excess nitrogen accumulated during the dive.

- **Depth.** The deepest point reached during the dive, no matter how briefly you stayed there. This means that even if you had only planned to go to 30 feet (9 metres), but you became interested in an artifact lying at 40 feet (12 metres) and go to investigate it—even briefly—the depth you use in calculating your dive is 40 feet or 12 metres (Figure 4-8, facing page).

- **Bottom Time.** The amount of elapsed time from the start of your descent to the time you begin your direct ascent back to the surface (see Figure 4-8).

- **Actual Bottom Time (ABT).** The actual amount of time a diver spent under water on a repetitive scuba dive.

- **Residual Nitrogen Time (RNT).** Excessive nitrogen pressure still residual in the diver at the beginning of a repetitive dive, expressed as minutes of exposure at the planned repetitive dive depth.

- **Total Bottom Time (TBT).** The time divers must use to calculate their new repetitive group designation at the end of a repetitive dive. Calculated as *Actual Bottom Time (ABT) + Residual Nitrogen Time (RNT) = Total Bottom Time (TBT)*.

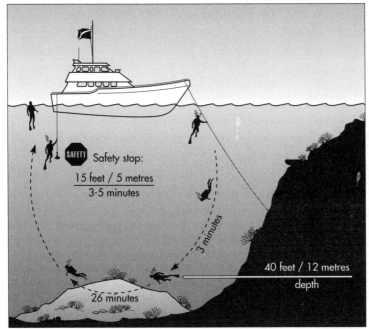

Figure 4-8 Depth and bottom time.

THE DIVE TABLES

When you begin to use the tables, it easiest to think of them as three separate tables, each with its own function.

■ *Table 1: The No-Decompression Limits Table.* This table has two basic functions. First, it shows divers how long they may stay at a certain depth without being affected by decompression sickness. Second, once the dive is made it assigns a group designation letter depending on how long a diver has been at a depth.

■ *Table 2: The Surface Interval Table.* This table is used when divers make repetitive dives. This table gives divers credit for the time they have spent "off gassing," or breathing excess nitrogen from the body, which then lowers their group designation letter.

■ *Table 3: The Residual Nitrogen Times Table.* This table is used to calculate Residual Nitrogen Time (RNT). It shows how much nitrogen a diver still has in the body before beginning the repetitive dive, and gives the adjusted no-decompression limit for the next dive.

Let's now take a look at how to put all of the tables and terminology into action by showing how to plan a no-decompression, repetitive dive with the dive tables.

TABLE 1: The No-Decompression Limits Table

TABLE 1 — No-Decompression Limits and Repetitive Group Designation Table For No-Decompression Air Dives

HOW TO USE TABLE 1: *Find the planned depth of your dive in feet or metres at the far left of Table 1. Read to the right until you find the time (minutes) you plan to spend at that depth. Read down to find the Group Designation letter.*

DEPTH feet	metres	Doppler No-Decompression Limits (minutes)	A	B	C	D	E	F	G	H	I	J	K
10	3.0		60	120	210	300							
15	4.5		35	70	110	160	225	350					
20	6.0		25	50	75	100	135	180	240	325			
25	7.5	245	20	35	55	75	100	125	160	195	245		
30	9.0	205	15	30	45	60	75	95	120	145	170	205	
35	10.5	160	5	15	25	40	50	60	80	100	120	140	160
40	12.0	130	5	15	25	30	40	50	70	80	100	110	130
50	15.0	70		10	15	25	30	40	50	60	70		
60	18.0	50		10	15	20	25	30	40	50			
70	21.0	40			5	10	15	20	30	35	40		
80	24.0	30			5	10	15	20	25	30			
90	27.0	25				5	10	12	15	20	25		
100	30.0	20				5	7	10	15	20			
110	33.0	15					5	10	13	15			
120	36.0	10							5	10			
130	39.0	5								5			

GROUP DESIGNATION: **A B C D E F G H I J K**

Figure 4-9   Table 1—The No-Decompression Limits table.

The first function of Table 1, **No-Decompression Limits and Repetitive Group Designation Table for No-Decompression Air Dives**, which we refer to as the No-Decompression Limits table, is to show divers how long they can stay at certain depths before taking in too much nitrogen to make a direct return to the surface. These limits are shown on the upper, rectangular shaped portion of the table (Figure 4-9). If you don't find the exact time in the table, round up to the next greater time.

The column in the far left shows depth in feet and metres. The next column over shows the Doppler No-Decompression Limits in minutes. You cross reference these numbers to find the maximum number of minutes you can spend at these depths. For example, if you're diving to a depth of 35 feet (10.5 metres), your maximum no-decompression limit at that depth is 160 minutes. If you're diving to 50 feet (15 metres), your maximum no-decompression time at that depth is 70 minutes, and so forth.

Now, it is unlikely that you would ever dive to a certain depth and remain exactly at that depth the entire dive. So, if the deepest point of your dive exceeds a certain No-Decompression Table depth you have planned for, go to the *next higher* number on the table. For instance, if you had planned to go to 50 feet (15 metres) and the deepest point you reach on your dive is actually 52 feet (16 metres), you refer to 60 (18) on the table.

The next step in using the tables is to find your maximum allowable bottom time at that depth. Using the same example, if you dive to 52 feet (16 metres), refer to 60 or 18 on the table and then move to the right and find your Doppler limit at that depth. It is 50 minutes (see Figure 4-10, step 1). So, for a dive to 52 feet (16 metres), your maximum bottom time at that depth is 50 minutes. Recall that your bottom time starts when you descend and ends when you begin your direct ascent.

While the Doppler No-Decompression Limits refer to the maximum time you can spend at certain depths, the numbers to the right of these columns correspond to the time you actually spend diving. In other words, you would rarely dive for the maximum of 205 minutes at 30 feet (9 metres) just because that is the no-decompression limit. For example, you may more likely dive 30 feet for only 35 minutes.

This leads us to the second function of the tables. The letter designations you see at the bottom of Table 1 are used to indicate the diver's *residual nitrogen* after a dive. Every diver has a certain amount of dissolved nitrogen left in his or her body after each dive. This *group designation* letter is used by the diver to figure out how long a *surface interval* must be taken before making another dive; that is, how long the diver must stay out of the water before diving again.

Let's continue with our original example of a dive to 52 feet (16 metres) for 36 minutes. You would move in the 60 foot (18 metre) depth bar to the entry for 36 minutes. Because there is no 36 minute limit, you must refer to the *next higher* time limit which is 40 minutes (see Figure 4-10, step 2). Now read straight down. You will see that the group designation for this cross reference is group "G." So, if you make a dive to 52 feet (16 metres) for 36 minutes, which rounds up to a 60 foot (18 metre) dive for 40 minutes, you are said to be a "G-Diver" (Figure 4-10, step 3).

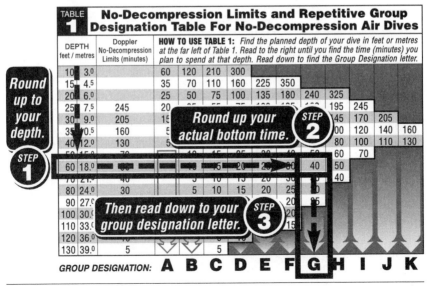

Figure 4-10 How to use Table 1.

So far you've learned how to stay within depth and time limits for no-decompression dives, and you've also learned how to find your group designation. Now we will look at what you do with this group designation, should you choose to make a repetitive dive.

TABLE 2: The Surface Interval Table

GROUP DESIGNATION: A B C D E F G H I J K

HOW TO USE TABLE 2:

Enter with the Group Designation letter from Table 1. Follow the arrow down to the corresponding letter on Table 2. To the left of these letters are windows of time. Read to the left until you find the times between which your surface interval falls. Then read down until you find your New Group Designation letter. Dives following surface intervals of more than 12 hours are not repetitive dives.

TABLE 2 — Residual Nitrogen Timetable For Repetitive Air Dives

REPETITIVE GROUP AT THE BEGINNING OF THE SURFACE INTERVAL

A	B	C	D	E	F	G	H	I	J	K
0:10 / 12:00*										
3:21 / 12:00*	0:10 / 3:20									
4:50 / 12:00*	1:40 / 4:49	0:10 / 1:39								
5:49 / 12:00*	2:39 / 5:48	1:10 / 2:38	0:10 / 1:09							
6:35 / 12:00*	3:25 / 6:34	1:58 / 3:24	0:55 / 1:57	0:10 / 0:54						
7:06 / 12:00*	3:58 / 7:05	2:29 / 3:57	1:30 / 2:28	0:46 / 1:29	0:10 / 0:45					
7:36 / 12:00*	4:26 / 7:35	2:59 / 4:25	2:00 / 2:58	1:16 / 1:59	0:41 / 1:15	0:10 / 0:40				
8:00 / 12:00*	4:50 / 7:59	3:21 / 4:49	2:24 / 3:20	1:42 / 2:23	1:07 / 1:41	0:37 / 1:06	0:10 / 0:36			
8:22 / 12:00*	5:13 / 8:21	3:44 / 5:12	2:45 / 3:43	2:03 / 2:44	1:30 / 2:02	1:00 / 1:29	0:34 / 0:59	0:10 / 0:33		
8:51 / 12:00*	5:41 / 8:50	4:03 / 5:40	3:05 / 4:02	2:21 / 3:04	1:48 / 2:20	1:20 / 1:47	0:55 / 1:19	0:32 / 0:54	0:10 / 0:31	
8:59 / 12:00*	5:49 / 8:58	4:20 / 5:48	3:22 / 4:19	2:39 / 3:21	2:04 / 2:38	1:36 / 2:03	1:12 / 1:35	0:50 / 1:11	0:29 / 0:49	0:10 / 0:28

NEW GROUP DESIGNATION ▶ A B C D E F G H I J K

REPETITIVE DIVE DEPTH ▼ ▼ RESIDUAL NITROGEN TIMES DISPLAYED ON REVERSE ▼

Figure 4-11 Table 2—The Surface Interval Table.

For most divers it is just not enough to dive once and then call off your dive day. In fact, scuba diving can be so captivating that it can sometimes seem like an imposition to have to return to the surface at all. Well, we all know by now that staying down over certain time limits is not safe, but it is comforting to know that you can safely build into your dive plan what are called *repetitive dives*.

When planning repetitive dives, refer to the triangle shaped part of the Tables which is headed **Table 2: Residual Nitrogen Timetable for Repetitive Air Dives,** we refer to this table as the Surface Interval Table. This is where your group designation becomes useful (Figure 4-11).

As a note, if your surface interval is less than ten minutes, you must consider both dives to be one continuous dive. If you are out of the water for twelve hours or longer, you are no longer subject to residual nitrogen times. Dives following surface intervals of less than ten minutes or more than twelve hours are not repetitive dives.

You will notice in Figure 4-11 that the group letters descend in order down the diagonal border of the table. To the left of these diagonal letter designations are various "windows" of time, such as 41 minutes to 1 hour and 15 minutes, or 0:41 to 1:15, which is located two windows to the left of the letter "G." Your *Surface Interval Time (SIT),* or your time spent out of the water between dives, will lie within one of these time windows.

Assume that you and your buddy decide to stay out of the water for around an hour and a half—time enough to have lunch and refill tanks. Your surface interval, then, would be 1:30. Using Table 2, move from your "Group G" designation to the left until you find the times between which one hour and thirty minutes lies. That would be 1:16 to 1:59 (see Figure 4-12, step 4). Now notice that while this time frame lies inside a horizontal bar, it is also part of a vertical column which drops down to another set of letters. These letters are aligned across the top of the lower part of Table 2, and the top of Table 3 which is on the back of your dive slate. To figure your residual nitrogen time, first follow down the column from your surface interval time. This will lead you to a new group designation letter, in this case "E" (see Figure 4-12, step 5).

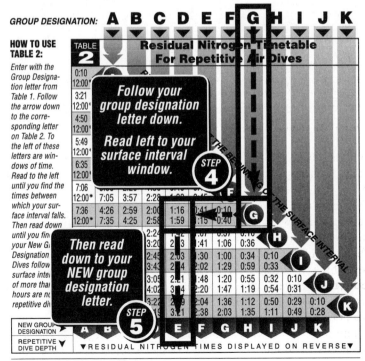

Figure 4-12 How to use Table 2.

TABLE 3: The Residual Nitrogen Times Table

TABLE 3	Residual Nitrogen Times (Minutes) — CONTINUED FROM REVERSE SIDE —										
NEW GROUP DESIGNATION ▶	A	B	C	D	E	F	G	H	I	J	K
REPETITIVE DIVE DEPTH — feet / metres	■ = ADJUSTED NO-DECOMPRESSION TIME LIMITS N/L=NO LIMIT										
10 / 3	39 / N/L	88 / N/L	159 / N/L	279 / N/L							
20 / 6	18 / N/L	39 / N/L	62 / N/L	88 / N/L	120 / N/L	159 / N/L	208 / N/L	279 / N/L	399 / N/L		
30 / 9	12 / 193	25 / 180	39 / 166	54 / 151	70 / 135	88 / 117	109 / 96	132 / 73	159 / 46	190 / 15	
40 / 12	7 / 123	17 / 113	25 / 105	37 / 93	49 / 81	61 / 69	73 / 57	87 / 43	101 / 29	116 / 14	
50 / 15	6 / 64	13 / 57	21 / 49	29 / 41	38 / 32	47 / 23	56 / 14	66 / 4			
60 / 18	5 / 45	11 / 39	17 / 33	24 / 26	30 / 20	36 / 14	44 / 6				
70 / 21	4 / 36	9 / 31	15 / 25	20 / 20	26 / 14	31 / 9	37 / 3				
80 / 24	4 / 26	8 / 22	13 / 17	18 / 12	23 / 7	28 / 2					
90 / 27	3 / 22	7 / 18	11 / 14	16 / 9	20 / 5	24 / 1					
100 / 30	3 / 17	7 / 13	10 / 10	14 / 6	18 / 2						
110 / 33	3 / 12	6 / 9	10 / 5	13 / 2							
120 / 36	3 / 7	6 / 4	9 / 1								
130 / 39	3 / 2										

HOW TO USE TABLE 3: Enter with the New Group Designation letter from Table 2. Next, find the planned depth of your repetitive dive in feet or metres at the far left of Table 3. The box that intersects the Repetitive Dive Depth and the New Group Designation will have two numbers. The top number indicates the Residual Nitrogen Time. The bottom number indicates the maximum Adjusted No-Decompression Time Limit for the next dive.

Figure 4-13   Table 3—The Residual Nitrogen Times Table.

The rationale behind Table 3, which we refer to as the Residual Nitrogen Times Table, is that even after a surface interval you still retain in your blood and tissues some nitrogen which has not yet come back out of solution (Figure 4-13). This excess, stored nitrogen in your body is referred to as *residual nitrogen,* and it requires you to factor in a time deficit when planning your next dive. In other words, you need to plan your next dive pretending that you have already been under water for a period of time, already taking on nitrogen.

Let's say you'd like to make your next dive to 40 feet or 12 metres for somewhere around 40 minutes. You will need to look at the left column of Table 3 where it says "Repetitive Dive Depth" and read for 40 feet or 12 metres (see Figure 4-14, step 6). Now cross-reference to your new "E-Diver" column. You'll find two numbers in this box— 49 and 81 (see Figure 4-14, step 7). The 49 minutes is your *residual nitrogen time* (RNT), the time you must assume you have already been absorbing nitrogen at that depth on your second dive. The 81 minutes is your *adjusted no-decompression limit,* or the total amount of time the Doppler no-decompression limits will allow you to spend at 40 feet. Your dive must be less than 81 minutes. This adjusted bottom time has only been calculated for the Doppler limits.

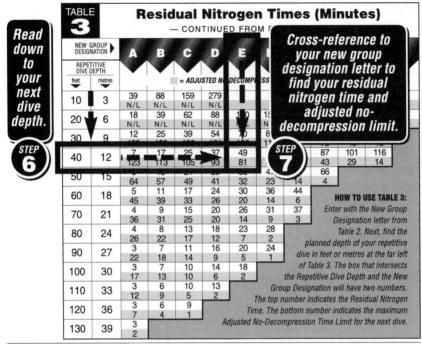

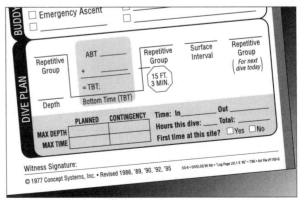

Figure 4-14   How to use Table 3.

REPETITIVE DIVES AND THE DIVE PROFILE

The Dive Tables are designed to allow you to make as many repetitive dives per day as you would like, as long as you remain within the Doppler no-decompression limits. Many divers make two, three or even four dives in one day. To keep track of their dives, divers use a dive *profile*. This is a simple graph which includes all the relevant information for recording no-decompression and repetitive dives. You and your buddy should always complete the dive profile on your DiveLog page (Figure 4-15).

Figure 4-15   The dive profile on your DiveLog page.

Use the profile to record the depth, bottom time and repetitive group from your first dive (Figure 4-16a). After your second dive to 40 feet or 12 metres for 40 minutes, chances are you'll want to go down yet again. In this case you'll have to come up with another group designation from which you can figure residual nitrogen time and plan your third dive. Do this by adding your *actual bottom time* of 40 minutes (which is the bottom time from your second dive) to your *residual nitrogen time* of 49 minutes (which we calculated from Table 3 after your first dive) to come up with a *total bottom time* of 89 minutes. Remember the calculation ABT + RNT = TBT. For this dive your bottom time is then 89 minutes (Figure 4-16b).

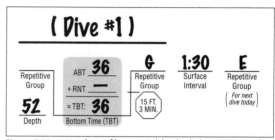

Figure 4-16a   Use the profile to record the depth, bottom time and repetitive group from your first dive.

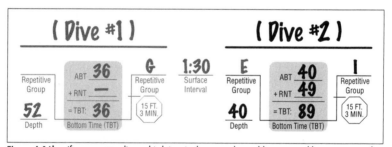

Figure 4-16b   If you want to dive a third time in the same day, add your actual bottom time and your residual nitrogen time from your second dive to come up with the total bottom time of your second dive. Then you can determine a new repetitive group for a third dive.

Returning to Table 1, the No-Decompression Table, move from your depth of 40 feet (12 metres) horizontally across to the next higher number above 89 minutes, which is 100 minutes (see Figure 4-17, steps 1-7). This gives you a group designation of "I." Again, go to Table 2, the Surface Interval Table, and follow the procedure for determining your surface interval and new group designation. Let's see what would happen if you used the same surface interval as last time—one hour and thirty minutes. Cross-reference from your group letter "I" to the time window 1:30 to 2:02. Then move down to your new designation as an "F-Diver." Now go to Table 3, the RNT Table. If you wanted to go down to 20 feet or 6 metres on a third dive, you will notice on the RNT Table that there is no adjusted no-decompression time limit in the 20 foot box. That is because there isn't any set no-decompression time limit for 10 or 20 feet (3 or 6 metres). You may also have noticed this in Table 1 under the column "Doppler No-Decompression Limits (minutes)." You will again notice that there is no set limit for 10, 15 or 20 feet. These depths are considered shallow enough to allow almost unlimited bottom time, even on a repetitive dive.

Two things make this repetitive dive plan successful. First, the *depths are moderate,* and second, the *deepest dive was done first and shallower dives were done as the day progressed.* Following these two general rules in repetitive dive planning will give you more flexibility with surface intervals and bottom times. If you plan deeper dives followed by shallower dives, and keep the depths of your repetitive dives moderate, you'll allow yourself longer bottom times and shorter surface intervals in general. It can be annoying and can really limit the day's activities if you use the tables unwisely.

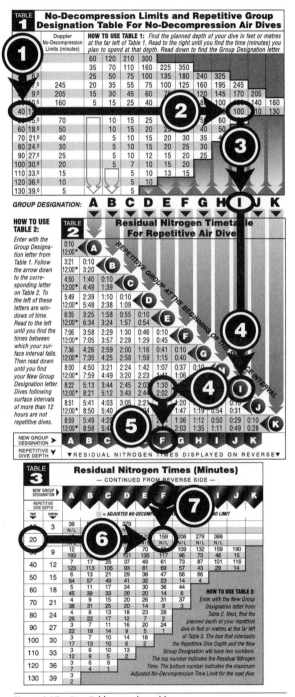

Figure 4-17   Dive Tables sample problem.

DIVE PLANNING

The reason for dive planning is, first, to plan safe dives and, second, to efficiently plan your day. If you know ahead of time what combination of depths and times for repetitive dives will be most efficient, you will be able to get the most benefit from your dive day (Figure 4-18).

> **If you know ahead of time what depths and times will be most efficient, you'll get the most benefit from your dive day.**

Figure 4-18   The reason for dive planning is, first, to plan safe dives and, second, to efficiently plan your day.

Note to Readers: From here forward we will be working out two actual dive plans and profiles. Closely follow along with your Doppler-adjusted Navy Dive Tables, and make notes on scratch paper if necessary.

If you and your buddy plan to do several dives, say three or four, during your dive day, you will want to do some pre-planning to determine the best combination of depths and times to get the most out of your day. Let's imagine, first, that you would like to go to a depth of about 58 feet or 17 metres and stay for about 48 minutes. When you go to Table 1 you find that the Doppler no-decompression limit for 58 feet or 17 metres (60 feet or 18 metres on the table) is itself 50 minutes, in which case it would be pushing the limits to do your 48-minute dive. So, it's back to the drawing board.

Suppose you have your heart set on this depth. Let's then try a more appropriate bottom time of 28 minutes. Following the table to the right and then down you find that diving at 58 feet (17 metres) for 28 minutes puts you in group "F." Now, since you will have been down for only 28 minutes you probably won't be ready for lunch yet when you surface, so you think a 30-minute surface interval would be sufficient before diving again.

Going down to Table 2 we find that after your first dive a surface interval of 30 minutes will keep you in group "F," the same designation you had after your first dive. Well, one of your objectives in planning repetitive dives is to *lower* your group designation. This always corresponds to less residual nitrogen left in your system, and therefore less residual nitrogen time deducted from your next dive. If you *were* only to stay out of the water for 30 minutes and then try to dive to, say, 55 feet (16 metres), your calculation using the tables will show only 14 minutes to spare for bottom time. Again, back to the drawing board.

This kind of thing will not happen every time you go diving. It is used as an example to show you how to approach a dive plan from the start. An experienced diver would already know that if he or she wanted to go to 58 feet (17 metres) on a first dive, a shorter bottom time and a longer surface interval would allow more flexibility.

Let's look at Table 2, the Surface Interval table, to see how much time you'd need to spend at the surface to get yourself down to a "D" or "C" designation. First, cross-reference from your horizontal "F" bar to the new group "D" column. Notice that this will require a surface interval of over 1 hour and 30 minutes. You decide you can live with this, but let's see how much bottom time that allows you at your destination of 55 feet (16 metres). By rounding up to 60 feet (18 metres) as your repetitive dive depth on Table 3, notice that you have 24 minutes of residual nitrogen time (RNT) and an adjusted no-decompression limit of 26 minutes. Being conservative with this limit would not allow as much bottom time as you'd like, so let's try a longer surface interval.

To get yourself down from "F" to a new group designation of "C," go back to the Surface Interval table and notice that you would have to spend at least 2 hours and 29 minutes at the surface, so you end up planning your surface interval for an even 2 hours and 30 minutes, and perhaps take an early lunch. Now let's go down to Table 3 again. Your RNT now will be 17 minutes, and your adjusted actual bottom time is 33 minutes at 55 feet (16 metres). Now you have allowed yourself another 30-minute dive, just like the first one.

However, this is not a conservative dive; 30 minutes is pushing the limits of a no-decompression time of 33 minutes. This brings up an opportunity to let the tables work in your favor. Do you suppose that whatever it is you're interested in at 55 feet (16 metres), say a wrecked ship, might be just as visible from 48 or 49 feet (14 or 15 metres)? If so, this would reduce your second No-Decompression Table depth from 60 feet (18 metres) to 50 feet (15 metres) and increase your no-decompression limit from 50 minutes to 70 minutes. Now, when you subtract your RNT of 21 minutes you have a comfortable adjusted no-decompression limit of 49 minutes to work with, making a 30-minute bottom time safer.

If you plan a third dive, you have to add in another factor: Your bottom time for the second dive will include the RNT from the first dive. Your group designation after the second dive will be figured on your actual bottom time from the second dive (30), plus your RNT from the first dive (21), giving you a *total bottom time* of 51 minutes. On the No-Decompression table you find that this gives you a group designation of "H" after diving to 49 feet (15 metres).

By now it would be a good idea to refill your tanks. Remember that you spent 2 hours and 30 minutes at the surface between your first and second dives. Suppose you'd like to shorten your surface interval this time. Let's work from what you'd prefer to do on your third dive and see if it's possible to fit in a shorter surface interval time.

This time you want to go to a depth no greater than 40 feet (12 metres), and you'd like to explore for 30 minutes if possible. Let's go down to Table 2 and move to the left of your "H" designation to an appropriate time window. If you think one hour and 30 minutes will do, go to the time frame of 1:07 to 1:41. This will give you a new group designation of "F." This means for a repetitive dive depth of 40 feet (12 metres) you will have an RNT of 61 minutes and an adjusted no-decompression time of 69 minutes. Remembering to be conservative with the tables, you consider a bottom time of 25 minutes. If, however, you can agree on a surface interval of just over 1:41—still shorter than your 2 hour and 30 minute interval after the first dive—you will have a new designation of "E." Your calculations will now show a slightly more flexible adjusted no-decompression limit of 81 minutes, in which case you might plan a 40-minute dive.

> Planning can be flexible, especially if you limit yourself to two dives per day.

Dive planning does not need to be strict and inflexible. In the every day reality of diving, planning can be flexible, especially if you limit yourself to two dives per day. For example, let's say you'd like to make your first dive to 50 feet (15 metres) and you want to stay for 30 minutes. Once you complete your first dive, there are two ways you can plan your second dive of the day.

At this time you can first decide how deep you want to go on the second dive and how much bottom time you would like to have, and then go to the Table 2 and figure out how much of a surface interval it would take to make the dive. The other route you could take is to plan the surface interval first and then see what you've allowed yourself for a repetitive dive. Whether you work backwards from proposed depths and times or forward from a surface interval, could depend either on how well organized you and your buddy are, or on conditions. For instance, if it's getting late in the afternoon and the temperature is dropping slightly, you may decide on a shorter surface interval and then just "go with" what the dive tables allow you.

But, remember that this is a time when you must be conservative, even though time may be pressuring you. Always make each dive such that you don't ever consider it as the last dive, but one in a series of lifetime dives.

Other Factors Affecting Nitrogen Absorption and Decompression

One reason it is advisable to be conservative with the dive tables is that there are additional factors which contribute to the formation of nitrogen bubbles in the blood and tissues. There are many things that can interfere with the efficient entrance and exit of nitrogen, including age, obesity, alcohol or drug use, medication, extreme heat or cold, loss of sleep, old injuries, extreme fatigue, proneness to blood clotting, and dehydration.

Altitude also affects decompression. When diving at altitude (1000 feet or 305 metres above sea level), your nitrogen absorption rate is different than at sea level because of the lower atmospheric pressure, and because diving at altitude is generally done in fresh water. Since the U.S. Navy tables were designed for use at sea level, special dive

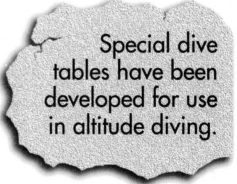

Special dive tables have been developed for use in altitude diving.

tables have been developed for use in altitude diving. You should be aware that they are based on theoretical models and that there is no standard high altitude table. Also, dive computers and depth gauges typically require time to adjust to altitude before they work accurately. When diving at altitude, the higher you go the more conservative you should be. Some SSI Dealers offer an *Altitude Diving* Specialty Course.

Flying after diving can be harmful for a diver supersaturated with nitrogen because airplane cabins are not pressurized to sea level pressure. To avoid problems, it is recommended that you wait 12 hours before flying in a pressurized airplane, and 24 hours if you plan to fly, or even drive, above 8000 feet or 2400 metres in a nonpressurized aircraft or vehicle. Divers who have been repetitive diving for several consecutive days should also make an extended surface interval longer than 12 hours, and may want to consider taking a day off in the middle of their diving week. Use this extra time for your sightseeing or your shopping. As an extra measure, it is a good idea to wait 24 hours before flying regardless of other considerations.

Using Computers for Repetitive Diving

There are many excellent dive computers on the market which can keep track of your vital diving information such as depth, time, surface interval, and ascent rate in order to monitor your nitrogen absorption. This information is calculated using a mathematical model and is not a precise measure of your absorbed nitrogen. They may also warn you if you go into decompression mode, or if you need to ascend slower.

Many experienced divers prefer to use computers because of the ease and flexibility they offer. Many dive profiles are actually what we call "multi-level" profiles, which means that a diver may actually dive at various depths throughout the dive. The dive tables are based on a straight profile, or a dive to one depth only. Most divers actually make multi-level dives, and the dive computer calculates each phase of the dive, giving the diver credit for the entire amount of time spent at shallower depths. Because computers calculate your own personal nitrogen level, divers should not share a computer. Each diver will have a slightly different profile with varying depths. Each dive buddy must use his or her own computer (Figure 4-19).

Figure 4-19 Because computers calculate your own personal nitrogen level, divers should not share a computer.

Computers can be very useful tools, but are also quite sophisticated and require training and practice in their use. They must only be used after familiarization with how they function, and divers must follow the manufacturer's recommendations for their brand and model of computer. See your SSI certified Instructor or SSI Authorized Dealer about taking a *Computer Diving* Specialty Course.

SUMMARY

By now in your training as an open water diver you've received the fundamentals. You might say that equipment plus proficient skills equals scuba diving. In this chapter you learned about a part of diving in which equipment and safe skills are inseparable: the U.S. Navy Dive Tables and their use in dive planning. You now know what decompression sickness is, and you know how to avoid it. The rest is up to you. Work with your instructor, ask questions, and work out the sample problems in your study guide. Like any other scuba skill, using the tables and planning your dives within the Doppler limits takes some work but really isn't very hard to do, and it will undoubtedly make you more comfortable as a diver and therefore make diving more enjoyable for you (Figure 4-20).

Where do we go from here? Now that you know *what* to do and *how* to do it, let's take our attention off of you and look at *where* you'll be practicing this newfound excitement called open water diving—the aquatic environment!

Figure 4-20   Using the tables and planning your dives will undoubtedly make you more comfortable as a diver.

The Aquatic Environment

Chapter 5: The Aquatic Environment

You might think of your open water course as a sequence of discoveries. By now you've discovered that you can live and function alongside the creatures of the water, simulating their fins and gills and seeing what they see. You've discovered things about your body that you may have never known, and you now know what precautions to take in order to allow your body to be able to function comfortably in this unfamiliar place.

The next discovery you will make is the inevitable goal of any learning experience. You are going to take your new skills and knowledge into the environment in which they are useful. You have learned about scuba so that you can take your new capabilities into the waters of the world. And this is the "hook" of scuba. If you have had doubts, or second thoughts of any kind at getting yourself involved in this sport, your mind will be changed by your first view of the dignity of an ancient coral reef whose halls play host to your games of hide and seek with brightly colored angel fish.

This adventure will begin with some necessary emphasis on the formation and makeup of water environments which harbor fascinating plants and animals. It is important for you to know a little about the history of the seas and inland water regions so that you'll have due respect and appreciation for these places. You would not go into a

Roman temple and chip off a piece of statue; neither should you break off pieces of coral just to display on your mantel at home. Remember that the oceans and waterways are places you need to adapt to—they are not your home. Always dive as a visitor, as the guest that you are in this new environment. As long as you do, you will be welcomed and have many opportunities to return.

SSI supports the ongoing efforts of the diving industry to protect our oceans, coral reefs and all aquatic environments for future generations. As an SSI diver, you too should accept the responsibility to protect these valuable resources which make the adventure of scuba diving not only possible, but also so captivating.

THE OCEAN ENVIRONMENT

The ocean contains a multitude of organisms, but at the same time it can be thought of as an organism itself. Though there is no way to know exactly what happened, we can speculate on the "birth" of the oceans and their evolution. The oceans' shallow waters move and are effected by the seasons, just as humans and animals are. Later in this chapter we will look at various inhabitants of the ocean, but for now let's discuss the ocean itself, how it developed, how it lives and breathes, and how we are connected to it.

OUR LINK WITH THE OCEANS

We only call the globe upon which we walk "Earth" because we are land inhabitants, and as the inventors of language it is our self-assigned privilege to call it whatever we want. If a whale, on the other hand, was capable of having "ideas" in our sense of the word, its idea of a name for this place would no doubt be different. The surface of this planet is actually made up of very little earth. It is in fact about 72% water (Figure 5-1).

Figure 5-1 The surface of this planet is actually made up of very little earth. It is in fact about 72% water.

Theories on how the oceans formed vary, but it is generally agreed that they are the product of condensing vapors which were left in the aftermath of the cosmic fireworks which began the formation of Earth, and the volcanic activity which continued for ages during the early history of Earth. As the earth cooled, these vapors condensed and fell as torrential rain, collecting in the low spots of this young planet. These rains continued until the oceans contained their current volume of nearly 1.5 billion cubic kilometres of water—a lot of water!

As these rains fell they washed minerals into the depths. Also, volcanic activity continued under water as well as on land, and what we now know as the oceans became receptacles for huge amounts of minerals. This resulted in the high degree of *salinity* that is characteristic of the oceans' salt water. Even though sea water tastes very salty, the salinity is actually only about 3.5%. But this salinity is made up of a high concentration of nutrients which forms the basic food for the multitude of plants and animals that inhabit the seas.

It is ironic that divers are entering a new and unfamiliar environment when they go diving in the ocean. Since all known fossil records tell us that the oceans were the original environment for animals, land animals actually evolved from water ancestors. Though we are talking about a span of 2 to 3 billion years since that early origin, we are in a sense revisiting our original birthplace when we explore the ocean.

The ocean remains today an extremely important source of life in that it is the home for many of the first links in the earth's food chain. Photosynthesis in plants creates oxygen in the oceans just as it does on land, and this initiates the process of creating organic nutrients which serve to feed more complex organisms, which in turn are fed upon by larger organisms, and so on. Animal waste and plant and animal decomposition complete the food cycle by replenishing the sea's basic nutrients and starting the chain of life all over again. It is estimated that the plant production in the oceans may be ten times more than that on land. More than 85% of the oxygen is produced by marine plants. Even the photosynthesis that takes place on land requires water which originates in the oceans.

In fact, inland waters are merely products of ocean water which have evaporated and condensed, and have then fallen as rain or melted from snowcaps and glaciers (Figure 5-2). Why, then, do inland waters lack the salt content of the oceans? There are a couple reasons for this.

Figure 5-2   Inland waters are merely products of ocean water which have evaporated and condensed.

First, water, as it evaporates, leaves minerals behind; when salt water evaporates, most of the salt stays in the ocean and fresh water is held by air until it falls as rain or snow. Second, any remaining salinity is removed by the process of freezing, which takes place in the polar and mountainous regions. As this ice melts, freshwater rivers and lakes are formed. Larger inland freshwater areas, such as the Great Lakes of the U.S., were formed over many thousands of years of warming temperatures which gradually melted glaciers. Ultimately, all of this fresh water flows back into the oceans to complete the cycle of water.

We are all linked directly or indirectly to the ocean. The ocean is the world's great caretaker. We all need to do our part to keep the oceans clean and free of pollutants; we must leave her in a pristine state if we expect to go on enjoying her natural beauty.

For us as divers, the oceans may be playgrounds, but playgrounds are only fun and exciting if we keep them clean and well maintained.

WATER MOVEMENT AND DIVING

So vast is the amount of water on the Earth, we are only recently gaining an understanding of such things as its life cycles, as mentioned above, and other phenomena such as the mechanics of water movement—basically how water "acts" when subject to particular conditions. Tides and currents, waves and surf all have some effect on divers and need to be understood in order to make dive planning more efficient and safe.

They also need to be understood so as to alleviate some natural fears. We are often overwhelmed by what we don't understand, but once you get to know the oceans and their natural rhythms there is nothing left to fear. Knowing why certain water movements come about, and how to respond to them, will eliminate the mystery.

TIDES AND TIDAL CURRENTS

The tide is an example of a wave, but it is the largest example on earth and the most dynamic water movement worldwide. Its wavelength, in fact, is half the circumference of the earth. The force that originally acts on the water to create tide is the gravity of the moon and sun, primarily the moon, pulling at the side of the earth nearest the moon. The centrifugal force of the earth's rotation pulls at the water in the opposite direction from the moon's pull. What results is a fairly steady-state "bulge" of water on the earth's surface (Figure 5-3). This gravitational/centrifugal force has a rubber band effect in that the water on the opposite side of the earth bulges in proportion to the gravity side.

The bulge seems to roll across the surface as the earth rotates and the moon orbits. But, as you will soon learn about waves, it is not the water that moves forward, it is the wave-creating *energy* that moves forward; similarly, it is the bulge of tide that moves forward, not the water in the bulge.

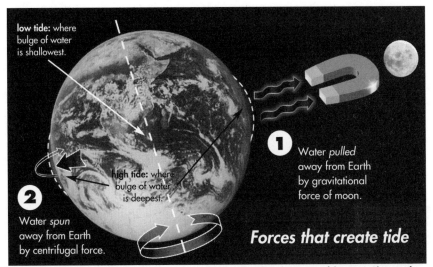

low tide: where bulge of water is shallowest.

1 Water *pulled* away from Earth by gravitational force of moon.

high tide: where bulge of water is deepest.

2 Water *spun* away from Earth by centrifugal force.

Forces that create tide

Figure 5-3   The force that originally acts on the water to create tide is the gravity of the moon. The centrifugal force of the earth's rotation pulls at the water in the opposite direction from the moon's pull. What results is a fairly steady-state "bulge" of water on the earth's surface.

When this bulge approaches a coastline, the water level rises and engulfs a greater portion of the shoreline than before. This vertical increase in water level is called *high tide*. At the same time the bulge is located at one area of the globe, the water which is pulled away and into the bulge leaves behind areas of *low tide* (Figure 5-4). Naturally, when this drop in water level occurs on a coastline, more of the shore is exposed. When the tide changes direction there is a period of no vertical movement in water level, and this is called the *stand*.

High Tide

Low Tide

Figure 5-4   This vertical increase in water level is called high tide. The water which is pulled away and into the bulge leaves behind areas of low tide.

Tides will enter into your dive planning. Near shore, the best time for diving would probably be during periods of minimal exchange of water between the tides. However, if you are going to make a very shallow dive on the open coast, the best time to go is at the peak of high tide to give greater depth and to reduce surge. One instance when you may want to enter during low tide is if you are snorkeling; low tide will maximize your effective time under water. The extent of tidal interchange may also have a considerable affect on the visibility.

Tidal Currents

The water which constitutes the tidal bulge is lifted, but does not move forward. However, as the tide moves across the face of the earth it creates a kind of "wake" which follows. This is called a *tidal current*. As tide comes to shore, a *flood current* follows. As the tide moves outward from shore, an *ebb current* follows. The period between the currents when no movement occurs is called *slack time*. Though the tidal currents and the slack time are related to the tides and the stand, they do not occur at the same time.

Tidal currents are of more interest to divers than the tides themselves. The currents cause water movement toward and away from shore, which can affect divers' entries and exits and can cause resistance for a diver swimming in the opposite direction of the current. This is especially critical in mouths of bays and lagoons. Tidal currents can also combine with other, more localized water movements, causing conflict which may result in unsteady waters.

It is, of course, always a good idea to dive in waters as calm as possible, and concerning tidal currents, this would ideally be during slack time. In most parts of the ocean, tidal currents will not figure into dive planning as much as more localized water movements such as waves and surf.

OCEAN CURRENTS

Another example of water movement on a global and/or local scale is ocean currents. These are caused by the sun heating different areas of the earth with varying intensity, combined with the effect of the rotation of the earth, resulting in different water temperatures. The water nearer the equator is warmer.

At the surface there are permanent oceanwide currents, or "streams." The six major streams are located such that there is one in each hemisphere of the Pacific, Atlantic, and Indian Oceans. These currents transplant warmer waters northward or colder waters southward along the coasts. This explains the presence of subtropical plants and animals off Florida and southern Japan, while Southern California is bathed by cold temperatures.

Thermoclines

Because dense, cold water tends to sink underneath warm water, layers of various temperature are found at different depths. The boundaries between these layers are called *thermoclines* (Figure 5-5). There are areas of sharply changing temperatures within a relatively narrow depth range. This occurs in all water bodies, and in the oceans thermoclines form at depths which often concern the sport diver, especially while diving in nontropical waters. Below the top 600 feet (183 metres) or so the temperature stays about the same much of the year, but at various layers above this depth temperatures may fluctuate considerably, and divers must therefore incorporate local temperatures into their dive planning. Waters in the shallowest depths may change by 4 to 5 degrees overnight in some areas.

Figure 5-5   Thermoclines.

Also of concern to sport divers are the periods of colder waters cycling downward. During the winter and summer months oceans and temperate lakes usually remain stratified with a fairly stable thermocline at some depth, but during spring and fall the seasonal change results in sudden drops or increases in temperature at the surface. This surface water cools or heats, becoming more or less dense, and the colder water sinks to seek a level of water with the same temperature. Wind can also cause a mixing of water resulting in deeper water becoming warmer. This cycling of water is called *overturn*. While these changes are taking place, divers can actually feel temperature differences just by moving slightly to one side or another, or by ascending or descending a few feet.

In fresh waters the diver is very likely to experience sharp temperature differences from one temperature layer to the next, even when stratified, merely because of the small sizes and shallower depths of lakes as compared to oceans. You should keep in mind when freshwater diving that the temperature at the surface may be much warmer than the temperature at your destination depth. Use protective wear according to the temperature you will encounter at that depth, not according to what is adequate at the surface. The same applies for most nontropical ocean diving, and to a much more limited extent, to tropical diving.

WAVES AND SURF

Cold polar air acts the same way cold polar water does. It descends, travels toward the equator, then warms and rises, creating several cyclical flows worldwide. When this air movement is near the earth's surface we call it wind; and when wind comes into contact with water, water movement of particular interest to divers—waves and surf—is formed at the surface.

Waves

Waves are generated in one of two ways: by wind, or by seismic activity on or near the ocean floor. By far the most common cause of waves is wind.

All wind waves are formed the same way. To imagine how waves are formed, first imagine a smooth water surface (Figure 5-6). As the wind comes into contact with the water, the friction of that contact lifts up small ripples in the water. The ripples slope upward and create a larger area against which the wind continues to blow. This increases the area of resistance that the wind can act upon, and larger and larger wavelets and waves are formed.

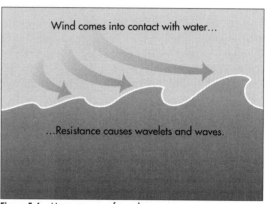

Figure 5-6   How waves are formed.

Three things determine how big the waves will get: 1) How hard the wind blows (velocity); 2) How long the wind continues to blow (time); and 3) Over what distance the wind continues to blow unimpeded (the *fetch*). The longer and harder the wind blows, the larger the waves become. The longer the fetch, the further the wave action will be extended.

The three factors mentioned above determine the height of waves, and wave *height* is related to *wavelength*. Wavelength is measured from the wave's *crest* to the crest of the next wave, with the wave *trough* lying between. The height of the wave is related to the wavelength at a ratio of about 1:7. That is, if the wavelength is 7 feet (2.1 metres), the height will range around 1 foot (.3 metre). If the wavelength is 21 feet (6 metres), the height will range around 3 feet (1 metre). The *period* of a wave is the time it takes for a wave to pass a fixed point, and as such is related to wavelength.

When a wave reaches a height that sets the water at a considerable angle from the horizontal, it either collapses under its own weight or, in the case of a strong wind, the top is blown off, creating the condition we call *whitecaps*. In open waters, as larger waves break, smaller ones form in the trough. Or waves from different directions mix together, and eventually a somewhat regular pattern of larger groups of waves followed by smaller groups forms beyond the area of the fetch. This continual pattern is known as *sea*.

Sometimes a relatively stable sea will be disturbed by wave energy coming from conflicting directions, resulting in a sea that essentially moves in two or more different directions. This is known as *confused sea*, and is often the cause of sea sickness—even affecting the "old salts" at times.

Seismic waves originate differently than wind waves. If there is a geological plate shift or some kind of volcanic disturbance under water, a sudden rise or collapse in the earth's crust on the ocean floor causes the water above to follow suit. A sudden void results on the water's surface, and it is immediately filled in by surrounding water. This sets up a chain reaction which perpetuates energy, resulting in long period/long wavelength waves. When such waves are predicted to arrive at a coastline site, monstrous waves can result. *No diving should take place during this time.*

No matter what the origin of waves, what sets a continual wave action in motion is the *energy* which results from the building up and collapsing of waves. In deep water, the water particles in waves at a given site actually move forward very little, but move primarily up and down in the same spot in a circular pattern. Instead of water moving forward, the energy is transferred forward by one wave to the next, and so on. It is the energy which moves forward, not the water in the waves themselves (Figure 5-7). Think of the action of a length of rope you

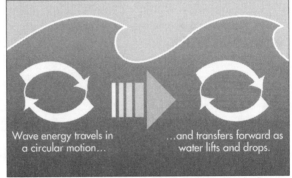

Wave energy travels in a circular motion...   ...and transfers forward as water lifts and drops.

Figure 5-7   It is the energy resulting from the building up and collapsing of waves that moves forward, not the water in the waves themselves.

hold at one end and then whip. A wave travels down the rope, but the rope stays in the same place. What travels is energy, not the rope. Electricity moving through a wire demonstrates the same principle.

Wave energy can travel for long distances and result in waves of varying size and strength. The energy only slows and refracts when something interrupts it. One way this can happen is when wave energy comes into contact with the ocean bottom near the shoreline. This is what causes the water movement we call *surf.*

We will discuss surf more in depth shortly, as surf can be of significant concern to the diver making shore entries and exits. First we'll look at some of the things boat divers need to be concerned with regarding water movement.

Entries and Exits When Boat Diving

For the most part, boat captains will exercise caution in locating an area with relatively calm water. Nevertheless, there are different water conditions in different regions, and those conditions plus the personal preferences of boat captains will dictate what entry and exit techniques you use. Be alert for these during your pre-dive briefing.

Regardless of other factors, when boat diving in the open water there are some general rules to follow in every case. Boats rise and fall with the motion of waves and swells. When entering or exiting a boat using a ladder or dive deck, mount or dismount when the boat dips into a wave trough. It is important to hold on when entering the boat because while your equipment feels weightless in water, as soon as you emerge from the water it will weigh you down and you may instantaneously feel the full weight of your body and equipment transferred to your arms. To shift your center of mass, lean forward slightly and offset this weight.

Keep your equipment on until you are safely on deck (Figure 5-8). The only exceptions to this include removing fins to climb a ladder, removing your weight belt to make you more positively buoyant, and removing equipment and handing it up if instructed to do so by your boat captain. Ideally, take these precautions in case you accidentally slip back into the water: Keep your mask in

Figure 5-8   Keep your equipment on until you are safely on deck.

place so you can see, your regulator or snorkel in place so you can breathe, and your BC inflated so you can float.

If you would like to learn more about diving from boats, especially in high seas, ask your local SSI Dealer about a Specialty Course in *Boat Diving*.

■ *Avoiding Seasickness.* If you are susceptible to seasickness, ask a diving physician for medication, and also inform your group leader so that you can enter the water as soon as possible when you reach your destination. By confirming your plan, assembling your equipment, and preparing to dress before arriving at your dive site, you can minimize the time spent on deck once the boat is anchored.

Surf

Past a fetch area, wind-generated waves begin to flatten and become the mild, steady back-and-forth motion known as *swells*, and the wave energy continues to move forward. When this line of energy comes into contact with the bottom near the shoreline it drags and slows, but its velocity at the surface continues unabated. This results in a steepening of the wave and shorter wavelengths. When the steepness of the waves exceeds a certain angle, the tops of the waves collapse and the waves *break*. At this point the water particles move toward the beach. These breaking waves are what we

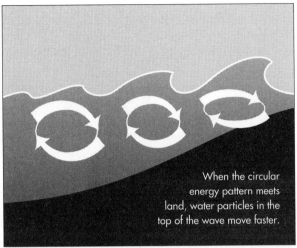

When the circular energy pattern meets land, water particles in the top of the wave move faster.

Figure 5-9   Breaking waves are what we call *surf.*

Figure 5-10   The movement of water returning from shore back to the ocean is called the backwash.

call *surf* (Figure 5-9). The movement of water returning from shore back to the ocean is called the backwash (Figure 5-10).

Since the line of energy travels toward the beach over fairly even lengths of shoreline in certain places, you'll sometimes see a pattern or series of waves parallel to shoreline. When surf is very powerful and steady, this pattern can form a hollow space under the crest resulting in the "tube" or "pipeline" of surfing fame.

There are three types of *breakers*: When the wave breaks slowly and spills evenly over the top, it is a *spilling breaker* (Figure 5-11a); when the water curls over and breaks all at once in a crash, it is a *plunging breaker* (Figure 5-11b); when the water peaks up and spouts, it is a *surging breaker* (Figure 5-11c). This happens in areas where there is an abrupt change at shoreline without a gradual approach, such as rocky cliffs or a very steep beach where the waves crash against a nearly vertical shore.

The area between the points at which the largest and smallest waves break is called the *surf zone* (Figure 5-12).

Figure 5-11a When the wave breaks slowly and spills evenly over the top, it is a spilling breaker.

Figure 5-11b When the water curls over and breaks all at once in a crash, it is a plunging breaker.

Figure 5-11c When the water peaks up and spouts, it is a surging breaker.

Figure 5-12 The area between the points at which the largest and smallest waves break is called the surf zone.

Entering and Exiting Surf

When entering or exiting from shore, the diver's primary concern is to avoid being knocked down and buffeted by surf and backwash. Once a diver has fallen down in a surf zone, large quantities of tumbling water can remove pieces of equipment and cause disorientation and serious injury.

Surf conditions vary widely throughout the world, so there is no absolute method for entry or exit that will cover all conditions.

> The first time you dive in any new environment, dive with a local SSI Dealer, Instructor or DiveCon.

The first time that you dive in this type of environment, or any new diving environment, it is recommended that you dive with a local SSI Dealer, Instructor or DiveCon. Also, when entering an unfamiliar area, if there are other divers nearby watch how they make successful entries and exits; and, as a general rule, always choose a place with the least water movement.

There are, however, several basic surf entries. One is used in more powerful breakers and/or when entering from a rocky of irregular shore. The other is used in even surf conditions where the approach to surf line slopes gently and is not rocky or irregular. First of all, waves usually enter shore in a pattern: a larger set of waves followed by a smaller set, and vice versa. Observe these sets and time your entries and exits to coincide with a smaller set.

If the surf is large enough to cause loss of balance, you'll follow a procedure that will get you into the water safely and past the surf zone quickly. With your mask and fins already on, your regulator in place and your BC inflated, interlock arms with your buddy, hold your mask in place and then shuffle backwards or sideways into the water until you are deep enough to swim (Figure 5-13). Watch the surf, and when it is about to break, stop and brace yourselves against it, then use the

Figure 5-13 If the surf is large enough to cause loss of balance, shuffle backwards until you are deep enough to swim.

backwash to help move you into waist-deep water, and finally turn and swim out *under* or *through* the waves, not over them. Your objective is to avoid the concentration of power at the point where water breaks, to get beyond the surf zone, and, if possible, to let the backwash help you move outward. (As a safety precaution, this method is recommended for all beach entries, regardless of conditions.)

If the approach to the surf is smooth and slopes gently, and the surf consists of very gentle, regularly spaced swells, while holding your fins but wearing all other equipment, walk into the water until about waist deep. Then, using your buddy for assistance, either cross one leg over the other in a "figure 4" and pull the fins on one at a time, or lie back in the water with your BC inflated and put them on one at a time. Then place the regulator in your mouth and, when you and your buddy are ready, swim out through the surf line. (This method should only be done in very calm conditions.)

Exiting surf is often much easier than entering. On an even shore under gentle conditions, just swim near the bottom where water movement is minimal, or find a shoreward-moving current to help bring you in. Let the water wash you up to a place where you can stand up and remain stable, remove your fins and walk up.

Follow the same procedures in heavy surf or on an uneven shore, but in addition, be sure to keep all your equipment on and the regulator in your mouth, let the water wash you up until you touch bottom, then crawl to a point where you can safely stand up and remove your fins (Figure 5-14). Do not turn around and sit down; this is a

Figure 5-14 In heavy surf or on an uneven shore, crawl to a point where you can safely stand up and remove your fins.

sure position from which to be knocked down by breaking water. In either case, exit on an even beach and in an area of gentle surf whenever possible.

When choosing a dive site, stay away from rocky shores and heavy water action. Also avoid choppy offshore waters, the result of waves and currents entering shore from different directions and at different speeds. This interaction causes turbulence, which can reduce visibility and create unusually large waves.

Under water divers experience *surge*, the back and forth movement of water caused by the energy of waves. The bigger the waves, the stronger the surge. To avoid strong surge, move a little deeper.

Localized Currents

Localized currents, or currents that run near shoreline, are either one of two types. *Longshore currents* flow alongside shoreline and are generated by waves which approach shore at an angle and then are kept from immediately returning oceanward by other incoming waves. When waves hit the shoreline at an angle the water "glances off," but in certain areas it is held back by shoreward moving water, and what results is a steady, slow-moving current running parallel to the shoreline.

Any time waves reach shoreline, the water must return to the sea. This returning water creates a back current, or *rip current*. Depending on the size and frequency of waves approaching shore, the direction from which they contact the shore, and the shape of the shoreline, rip currents of varying direction and strength result.

This returning water will always follow the path of least resistance. A rip current may be channeled through a low point between two sand bars, or it could form a trough in a soft sandy area near a more solid bottom formation (Figure 5-15).

When waves enter a cove or a curved area of shoreline, the return-ing water may flow in two different directions forming a rip current (Figure 5-16). Water reaching a point on the bank, say, near the north end of the cove, will flow to the south. Water that meets the south bank will flow to the north. When the two flows meet, they will funnel together and form a rip cur-rent.

It is often possible to see where the rip current is by noticing where there are areas of no waves or lower waves in the surf line. Because the outward moving ener-gy of the rip current cancels out the incoming energy of the waves or surf, you may also be able to see foam on the surface that is moving away from shore.

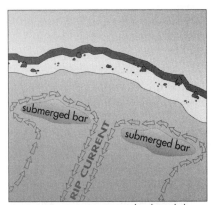

Figure 5-15 A rip current may be channeled through a low point between two sand bars.

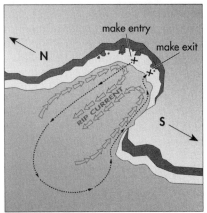

Figure 5-16 When waves enter a cove or a curved area of shoreline, the returning water may flow in two different directions forming a rip current.

Diving with Localized Currents

When shore diving, you can enter the rip current and allow it to float you out, then plan your exit so that you come back with the shoreward movement of waves. However, if you try to exit at the same point you entered, you will be facing into the rip current. When you use a rip current to carry you out, plan an exit that will allow you to avoid it on your way back. Any time you *do* find yourself facing into a rip current, turn and swim at a right angle or diagonal to it until you catch a shoreward water movement, or at least move out of the current's main force.

If waves approach an even shoreline straight on, rip currents which run opposite the direction of the waves may occur in several different places. If you get caught swimming into a rip current upon your return to shore you can escape it by swimming to one side or another. You will eventually swim around it.

You can predict the strength of a rip current by observing the conditions under which it must travel. If, for instance, it travels through a very narrow channel between submerged bars, it will move with an intense velocity. It would therefore be a good idea to avoid diving in the space between submerged bars. An easy way to recognize the location of submerged bars offshore is to notice where surf develops before getting to shoreline. This indicates wave energy coming into contact with shallow bottom formations offshore.

What people think of as undertow is either a rip current or the strong backwash from powerful surf.

While on the subject of rip currents, let's dispose of the myth about "undertow." What people think of as undertow is either a rip current or the strong backwash from powerful surf. The belief in a current that can sweep you out to sea, never to be seen again, is a fallacy. Rip currents do not extend very far beyond the surf zone. Besides that, it is usually a simple matter of moving to one side or the other to avoid being carried away from shore.

When boat diving in an area of localized current, you will usually be able to tell the direction of the current by the way the boat anchors. After anchoring, unless affected more by the wind than the current, the boat will tend to swing into the current away from the anchor, stretching the anchor line in the direction of the current as the water pushes at the boat. Watch objects floating beneath the surface of the water to estimate the current's speed. If it's extremely swift, you should move to a different area.

When you make a dive plan keep in mind that you make a safety stop of 3-5 minutes at 15 feet or 5 metres on every dive. You need to take this into consideration when boat diving. It is now best to swim against the current during your entire dive (or at least two-thirds of your dive) so that you will still be upstream of the boat when you surface after your safety stop. The best situation is to be able to ascend on the anchor or ascent line so that you will be at the boat when you surface (Figure 5-17).

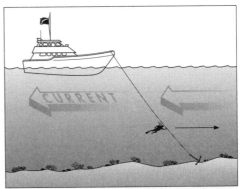

Figure 5-17 It is best to swim against the current during your entire dive so that you will still be upstream of the boat when you surface.

It is sometimes convenient to descend on an anchor line to get below the current before swimming. Many times a *trail line or current line* is also used in boat diving. This is a line extended off the stern of the boat for divers to hold onto before and after a dive. This is convenient in areas of current (Figure 5-18). Divers enter and hold onto the line while waiting for others so that they can all descend and begin the dive together. The trail line is also handy in exiting. It gives divers a stronghold before mounting a ladder or dive deck when located in a current.

Figure 5-18 A trail line is extended off the stern of the boat for divers to hold onto before and after a dive.

Another kind of boat diving allows the diver to move along with a longshore or offshore ocean current. In *drift diving* you simply float along with the current, and so does the boat. When you surface, the boat picks you up.

If you ever happen to drift downstream from your boat or exit point, don't panic. Stabilize yourself on the surface by getting positively buoyant and signal for help. Do not try to swim against the current. This will only exhaust you and complicate the problem. If possible, look for another exit point.

Always become aware of local water conditions, including the location and intensity of localized currents, before diving. You can consult tidal current tables, or ask an SSI Dealer or Instructor located in the particular area where you plan to dive.

UNDERWATER LIFE

The small portion of this planet on which we humans live is also inhabited by various animals. But because we dominate our environment, many of these other land dwellers have learned to hide from us and avoid contact with us. One of the most exciting things about exploring under water is that many life forms in water environments have not yet learned to fear us (and hopefully will never have to). What this means for the diver is that you often *will* see what you came to see. The sheer amount and variety of life in the oceans and waterways also contributes to the fact that you will surely see some spectacular beauty when you enter this home away from home.

Many dive sites throughout the world are considered marine parks and are protected by local laws. This protection helps keep these dive sites in pristine condition by protecting the coral and other aquatic marine life from hunters and collectors. However, with this protection comes regulation and responsibility. It is up to all divers to respect local laws and to help protect the corals and sea life in these parks.

Some aquatic wildlife are larger, such as the barracuda and ray, and some are hardly visible. Others are not so visibly active, such as the animal which lives inside the coral structure. The greatest variety of life will be visible near the coral reefs in equatorial waters. It is here that the food chain begins. Let's look at the coral reef and other ocean habitats, and also at some of the ocean's inhabitants, including some of the potentially dangerous specimens which you should be aware of, and later in the chapter we will examine some fresh water environments. If you are interested in learning more about marine life, contact your SSI Dealer about a Specialty Course.

MARINE PLANTS

There are some 350,000 plant species described to date, with over two-thirds of these living on land. Of the major divisions/ phyla in the plant kingdom, only the *algae* are well represented in the marine environment. These various algae, or Thallophyta, are either *benthic*, affixed to seabed or rock, or *planktonic,* floating. Algae in general is known as seaweed.

Many algae are microscopic, but some reach massive proportion, such as *kelp* (Figure 5-19). The mighty kelp forest is the cold water equivalent of the tropical coral reef. Kelp is a brown algae, often growing in dense beds in cold, temperate

Figure 5-19   Kelp.

waters. It is especially prevalent along the western Pacific Coast and presents an immense habitat for a multitude of other plants and animals.

MARINE ANIMALS

Of the more than one million species of animals throughout the world, only about 200,000 of these inhabit the oceans. Although this is still a large number to reckon with, they are represented by certain large categories of animals, and among these, the sport diver need only consider the most common and conspicuous phyla. These are the sponges (Porifera); hydroids, jellyfish, and corals (Coelenterata); various worm phyla, mainly the flatworms (Platyhelminthes) and the segmented worms (Annelida); snails, clams, and octopi (Mollusca); shrimps, crabs, and lobsters (Arthropoda); starfish, sea urchins, sea cucumber, and sand dollar (Echinoderma); and fishes and mammals (Vertebrata).

Sponges

Sponges are very simple animals characterized by bearing holes through which water circulates. They do not move except for opening and closing these holes, which is a very slow process. They vary in size, from nearly microscopic to large enough to envelope a dozen divers, and vary in shape from encrusting growths to ball-like and columnar shapes. Two common sponges are the basket sponge and tube sponge (Figure 5-20).

Basket Sponge.   Tube Sponge.

Figure 5-20   Two common sponges are the basket sponge and tube sponge.

Stinging Animals

The Coelenteratas, commonly called *hydroids*, are characterized by the presence of *nematocysts*, or stingers. The Stinging animals include the Portuguese Man-of-War (Figure 5-21a), purple coral, reef coral, jellyfish (Figure 5-21b), gorgonians, or sea fans, sea anemones (Figure 5-21c), and sea pansies. For the most part the stingers are located on the tentacles of the animals, and many are known to be venomous. The only species known to cause fatalities are various forms of the sea wasp, or box jelly-fish. These have batteries of tentacles which contain many millions of nematocysts.

Reef-building corals are known to exist in waters with a mean annual temperature of 72°F (22°C) and a minimum of 68°F (20°C). The extensive reefs of the Caribbean, South Pacific, Indian Ocean, and the Red Sea are thriving examples of the colonization of warm waters by these prolific animals.

Figure 5-21a   Portuguese Man-of-War.

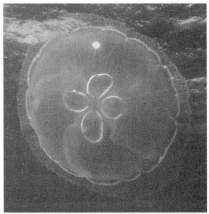

Figure 5-21b   Jellyfish.

Figure 5-21c   Sea Anemones.

THE CORAL REEF

Corals are colonial animals which construct skeletal structures of limestone, often forming extensive reefs in the shallower tropical seas where sunlight and warmer waters prevail (Figure 5-22). Coral animals, or *polyps*, attach permanently to a surface such as a rock face, and slowly build around themselves the protective structures and networks we see as the coral reefs. These may form as deep as 250 feet or 80 metres, although the majority of the species live at much shallower depths. Most of the healthy coral reefs in existence in the oceans were probably first formed around

Figure 5-22   Corals form extensive reefs in the shallower tropical seas where sunlight and warmer waters prevail.

200-300 million years ago, and they have persisted throughout the ages because the delicate balance in nature has kept the ocean waters clear and unpolluted.

As well as simply being beautiful to look at, the reef serves a variety of functions. It offers a home and protection for many species of animals. It is also a source of food for some. As these animals eat the coral, the residue becomes sand. The corals also harbor important algae called zooxanthellae. The algae provide needed oxygen for the coral, and the coral gives off carbon dioxide which the algae in turn need.

> To avoid injuring the coral, always maintain neutral buoyancy and practice good buoyancy control over reefs.

Some corals can be brittle, and some are capable of inflicting abrasions or cuts. These corals are also easily damaged by careless divers who kick corals with their fins, or hit the reefs with their tanks. To avoid injuring yourself or the coral, always maintain neutral buoyancy and practice good buoyancy control over reefs. It is also recommended that you stay a safe distance from the reef to avoid damage. It is best to appreciate the reefs with the eyes rather than the hands. Simply touching the corals may remove some of their protective mucous coating, making them susceptible to injury or infections.

Of the many varieties of coral, we will only look closely at a few which are most common and that you are most likely to see. They fall into two general categories: hard and soft corals. After looking at a few examples of coral, we will cover some of the other varieties of life forms which inhabit the coral reef.

Hard Corals

Among the more eye-pleasing of the hard corals is **elkhorn** coral (Figure 5-23a). It forms a major portion of the reefs, and is seen in great quantity particularly in the Caribbean. It is very sharp, and you can easily cut yourself if you come into contact with it. The **staghorn** coral grows similar to the elkhorn, but is more cylindrical (Figure 5-23b). The **brain** coral is one of the more intriguing sights in the coral reef (Figure 5-23c). Opening in floral bursts which cling closely to rocks and other hard surfaces is the **star** coral (Figure 5-23d). The **fire** coral is so named because of both its upward plumes of "flame," and because it can inflict a burning sting if you touch the nematocysts (Figure 5-23 e & f). It is not actually a coral, but a hydroid. Keep your distance from fire coral. A hard coral which may give the illusion of being soft is the **lettuce leaf**.

A. Elkhorn Coral.

B. Staghorn Coral.

C. Brain Coral.

D. Star Coral.

E. Fire Coral.

F. Nematocysts.

Figure 5-23   Hard Corals.

Soft Corals

The gorgonian corals are soft and flexible. Among the most beautiful soft corals is the sea fan, which takes different forms at different depths (Figure 5-24). In shallower waters its height ranges from 12 to 24 inches (30 - 60 cm). The deepwater sea fan can get huge, sometimes ten feet (3 metres) across. Black and red coral are other examples of the soft corals.

Figure 5-24   Among the most beautiful soft corals is the sea fan.

Worms

What we normally think of as worms are not what you're likely to see under water. Probably the most conspicuous, and those that are favorites of underwater photographers, are the segmented worms which construct sand or calcareous tubes. These include the feather duster and the Christmas tree worms, sometimes called *tube worms* (Figure 5-25). Since they live in tubes, the diver normally only views the filter-feeding end of the worm. This end looks like a number of concentric, sometimes brilliantly colored or patterned rings. When viewed from the side they look like a miniature evergreen.

Figure 5-25   Christmas tree worms.

Mollusks

The most archaic form of the mollusk is the *gastropod*. There are more than 35,000 species known, which include snails, abalone, and conch. The *bivalves*, or two-shelled mollusks include the clam, oyster, mussel, and scallop. There are nearly as many species of bivalves as there are gastropods.

The *cephalopods*, more commonly known as the squid and octopus, are the largest of all known invertebrates. They are highly developed, having several arms and the ability to move by forcing water out of a deep mantle cavity.

Crustaceans

The group called *arthropod* includes insects, but also includes a class of animal of more interest to the diver, the crustaceans— lobsters, crabs, and shrimp (Figure 5-26). They are characterized by jointed appendages and external skeletons. Where local regulations allow the harvest of these animals,

Figure 5-26   Lobster.

the diver must be familiar with minimum sizes, numbers allowed, hunting hours and seasons, and must respect these local regulations.

Echinoderms

Sea stars, brittle stars, sea urchins, sand dollars, and sea cucumbers all belong to the group of animals known as the Echinoderms. This entire group is marine, with no known fresh water examples. They have a five-sided radial symmetry with an internal skeleton of small bones. The urchins and cucumbers are prized as a food source in some cultures.

Vertebrates

The *vertebrates*, fishes and mammals, are well known and are the most visible life forms in the open waters. For the interest of the diver we will look at examples divided by environment. There are estimated to be 40,000 species of fish, so we are naturally limited to including some of those you are most likely to see. If you are particularly interested in sea life, it is recommended that you talk to your SSI Dealer or Instructor or do some reading about local varieties before you go diving. If you plan on hunting, pay special attention to local regulations governing licensing, limits, gaming seasons, and marine parks. Mammals, of course, are fully protected.

Pay special attention to local regulations governing licensing, limits, gaming seasons, and marine parks.

Tropical Reef Fish

The reefs are truly amazing in their wealth of life. While the corals themselves are alive, they are inhabited by a vast range of life forms, from microorganisms to large pelagic fish. Most commonly seen are the smaller reef fish which make the caves, crevices, and hollows of the reef their home and shelter. An interesting aspect of life in the reef is that its inhabitants are territorial; larger fish will claim and control a portion of the reef with dimensions of several feet, and even the tiniest fish control areas of perhaps only a few inches. Since the Caribbean is the most often-visited tropical resort area for divers, we will feature the following fish which are the most commonly seen when diving at Cozumel, Roatan, Belize, Cayman, and the Bahamas.

Some of the most common and often seen groups are the varieties of angel fish. They are also some of the most beautiful, and as such are best appreciated by the eye—they are not considered edible. There are four common types of angel fish. The Gray Angel is distinguished by its spotted gray markings. It is a friendly fish and will occasionally allow a diver to pet it. Another of the angels is the French Angel which is black with bright yellow scales, easily distinguished from its neighbors.

Figure 5-27   Queen Angel.

The Blue and Queen Angels are a little harder to tell apart. The Queen is distinguished by the "crown" marking above its head (Figure 5-27).

The butterfly fish is often confused with the angel. The Puerto Rican Butterfly is also known as the "banded" butterfly. Another variety is the Spot Fin. Butterfly fish are quite tame and have no apparent enemies.

Other colorful but inedible members of the reef population

Figure 5-28   Queen Trigger.

include the Rock Beauty, the Black Durgeon which is distinguished by bright purple lines at the dorsal and anal fins, the Queen Trigger, the Glasseye, the phosphorescent purple and yellow Fairy Basslet, and the tiny Squirrel Fish (Figure 5-28).

Other reef dwellers are considered edible. Among the most highly prized are the groupers. The grouper family includes the Nassau, the Tiger, and the Spotted. The grouper is cousin to the larger deep water Sea Bass.

The Parrot Fish is one of the greatest contributors to the reef (Figure 5-29). It eats the coral animal, and thereby creates sand as it gnaws away at the outer structure. It also eats algae and produces waste that is important to the reef ecosystem. The Parrot may or may not be edible, depending on its particular territory and diet.

Figure 5-29   Parrot Fish.

The snapper is a quite popular fish for the table. This family includes the famous Red, the Yellowtail, Dog, and Grey, to name just a few.

The jack family makes up a large part of the pelagic (free-swimming and non territorial) fish population which skirts the reef. They are large and powerful and can reach weights in excess of 100 pounds (45 kilos). The Amberjack and Horse-eye jack are two of the most famous jacks (Figure 5-30).

Some of the smaller varieties of fish you are likely to see swimming in schools include the Grunt, the Damselfish, and the Blue Chromis.

Figure 5-30   Horse-eye jack.

To help you identify and enjoy reef fish, many SSI Dealers teach *Marine Identification* Specialty Courses.

COLD WATER FORMATIONS

While the coral reef offers protection and food for warm water dwellers, the deeper cold water areas do the same for their inhabitants. Cold water bottom formations are mostly comprised of rock, and along some coastlines, kelp beds. Though not as colorful or as varied in life forms as the coral reefs, cold waters often offer a greater quantity of marine life with a view of some of the most exciting ocean creatures, including the marine mammals such as sea lions, seals, dolphins, and whales.

The kelp forests found in coastal areas of California, Alaska, and Japan, to name a few, offer very unique diving experiences. Kelp is abundant with life and is home to many of the kinds of oceangoing fish we meet most often at dinnertime: Halibut, Sole, and Turbot (Figure 5-31). Other fish commonly seen in the kelp forests include the bright orange Garibaldi, and a wide variety of rockfish.

Figure 5-31   Dover Sole.

Kelp is not difficult for the trained diver to move through if it is done slowly and carefully, without a struggle. However, a thorough orientation in kelp diving should precede any attempt at exploring this magical environment. Consult local dive stores in regions where kelp is abundant.

> Artificial structures such as oil rig platforms and ship wrecks serve as "reefs" in colder waters.

In areas where it grows to the water's surface, the kelp forms a "bed" which can be traveled across by using the *kelp crawl.* If you ever become entangled in kelp, simply stay calm, move slowly, and gradually disentangle yourself. Your buddy may be able to help.

Artificial structures such as oil rig platforms and ship wrecks serve as "reefs" in colder waters. They offer protection for smaller fish and therefore attract larger pelagic fish which come to feed. It is not uncommon to see Yellowtail Jacks, smaller species of tuna, bonito, mackerel, small barracuda, and possibly sharks.

POTENTIALLY HARMFUL MARINE LIFE

It should come as some comfort to you as a diver that you are not natural prey to anything that lives in the sea. Nevertheless, just as in any human venture or adventure there are risks involved, and one of those is the risk of injury by one of a number of marine animals. These injuries, however, are in nearly all cases avoidable. The creatures capable of inflicting injury will do so only defensively. They will react when surprised by being touched or having their territory invaded, or when taunted or molested. Both are defensive reactions. Being too large to be considered food for any marine animal, humans incur injury as a result of negligence, ignorance, or their own aggressive behavior.

In order to make you more aware of potential hazards, we'll look at some of the creatures capable of injuring divers.

By far the most common injuries are ones which occur when the animal is surprised and instinctively protects itself. This happens when a diver accidentally brushes against, grabs, or steps on something unseen, or something seen which is not known to be dangerous.

Of the creatures you may not see are the Sculpin, or "scorpion fish," and the Stonefish. The Sculpin is found in U.S. coastal waters and camouflages itself on the bottom. In fact, its appearance is much like that of a rock or shell when lying still. Its sting is not fatal, but painful, and should be treated by running hot water directly over the wound. The Stonefish looks much like the Sculpin, but is more dangerous (Figure 5-32). It is found mostly in the Pacific and is very difficult to spot; its camouflage makes it almost indistinguishable from the rocks and corals it inhabits. Treatment for a Stonefish sting includes hot water flushing, but the victim will also require immediate emergency care.

Figure 5-32 The Stonefish looks much like the Sculpin, but is more dangerous.

The eel is an animal you may see hiding in rocks, crevices, and coral formations (Figure 5-33). One of the most common is the Moray Eel. They are nocturnal and will be more free-swimming at

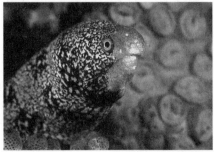

Figure 5-33 The eel is an animal you may see hiding in rocks, crevices, and coral formations.

night, so there is little danger of contact. However, if disturbed while at rest inside the dark enclosure where it lives, the eel may react by biting. Eels are normally quite shy and will avoid confrontation if possible.

Among creatures that do not appear to be dangerous at first glance are several of the phylum Coelenterata, including the Jellyfish and the Portuguese Man-of-War (see page 169— Figures 5-21 a & b). The Coelenteratas' nematocysts force poison into a victim when touched. The sting needs to be taken care of immediately: Leave the water, leave the stingers alone, douse the wound with vinegar or ammonia, or apply a commercial anti-sting solution, and get medical attention (Figure 5-34).

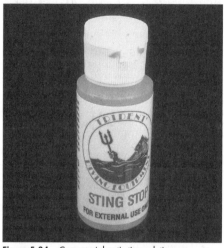

Figure 5-34 Commercial anti-sting solution.

The most dangerous Coelenterata is the Sea Wasp (Figure 35). The tentacles on the Sea Wasp can reach 10 metres in length. A six-inch length of tentacle has enough poison to kill an adult. If you are stung by these tentacles you will have extreme pain around the effected area. Within the first 90 minutes after the sting the victim can become unconscious and stop breathing. Treatment for a Sea Wasp sting includes applying copious amounts of vinegar or ice to the effected area and removing the tentacles very carefully. Apply a pressure bandage of vinegar or ice, monitor the vital signs and transport the victim to the nearest emergency medical facility.

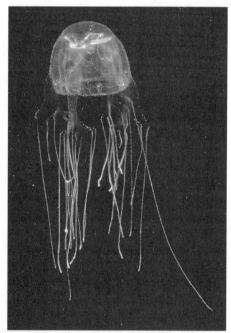

Figure 5-35 The most dangerous Coelenterata is the Sea Wasp.

The Cone Shell has a venomous stinger that hides inside its shell. Though Cone Shells do not attack, stings can result from careless handling and because divers mistake them for harmless sea shells. If you cannot positively identify a shell, do not pick it up. Treat Cone Shell stings by flushing with hot water. Also seek medical attention.

The sharp spines of the Sea Urchin are a common cause of puncture wounds (Figure 5-36). Care must be used to avoid breaking off any spines in the skin. Treat the puncture by immersing it in tolerable hot water to achieve pain relief. Gently remove any visible pieces of the spine and then scrub the wound with soap and water. If the spine is near a joint, or the wound is showing signs of infection, you must receive proper medical attention.

Figure 5-36   The sharp spines of the Sea Urchin are a common cause of puncture wounds.

When moving on the bottom, divers should watch for the inconspicuous ray. Several of the *stingrays*, including the Butterfly, the Bat, the Round Ray, and the Stingray, are capable of wounding an aggressive diver, or a diver who accidentally steps on one while it is inconspicuously burrowed into the sandy bottom (Figure 5-37). When disturbed or provoked they will swim away, but if attacked they will strike up with their tail and can drive a venomous barb located on the tail into an intruder. The sting will

Figure 5-37   The Stingray.

cause bleeding and swelling, and the poison can have serious side effects such as vomiting and faintness. If you are wounded by a ray get out of the water, immerse the wound in hot water, and get medical attention.

The Sea Snake is abundant in the Indian and Pacific Oceans, in the Persian Gulf and throughout Asia. Most species spend their entire lives in the open sea (Figure 5-38, next page). Though they are sluggish and not aggressive, they can bite if handled or provoked. The venom of sea snakes is powerful so the victim must be taken to medical services as soon as possible to receive antivenom.

A small but formidable foe is the Lionfish (Figure 5-39). It is nice to look at, but carries a powerful sting. Immediate treatment is a hot water flush, but medical attention may also be required.

Figure 5-38   The Sea Snake.

Another type of injury is the aggressive injury in which an animal takes a purposeful and willing part. An example of this sort is a shark bite. These injuries are rare. There is no doubt that some sharks are unpredictable and can be dangerous—but almost exclusively *when provoked* (Figure 5-40). They are fast and strong, and become very excited at the smell of blood in the water. Knowing these two facts—that

Figure 5-39   The Lionfish

they can be provoked and that they are excited by blood—are what film and documentary producers have employed to manufacture the myth of the ferocious shark. You can get even the tamest of sharks to react violently by *chumming* the water—tossing in bucketfuls of meat, intestines, and blood. But sharks are actually quite graceful, and can even be cowardly, often bolting away at sudden movement.

Figure 5-40   Some sharks are unpredictable and can be dangerous.

The most commonly seen sharks are the least aggressive. The Nurse and the Sand Shark are among these. More aggressive sharks include the Tiger, the Mako, and the Hammer-head.

Another large fish which doesn't quite deserve its reputation as a hostile predator is the Barracuda

Figure 5-41   The Barracuda.

(Figure 5-41). While it does have a fearsome appearance and does tend to stalk, it is actually very gentle and intelligent, and may follow a diver just out of curiosity. Barracudas have been known to be very friendly, in fact. They are, however, attracted by blood in the water just as sharks are, and care must be taken to avoid them when they are agitated.

We have only glossed the number of potentially dangerous marine life forms. For your purposes as a diver it is more important to know what you're likely to encounter when diving in a particular area. Many dangerous animals are indigenous to only one region. Ask your SSI Dealer or Instructor what to look out for in their waters, how to recognize them, how to avoid them, and what to do if you are injured.

FRESHWATER ENVIRONMENTS

Though ocean and coastal diving is popular, there are many inland, freshwater dive experiences worth investigating. Many divers live too far inland from salt water sites to be able to dive them exclusively, so they find some very diverse and interesting dive sites nearer to home. Inland dive sites include lakes, rivers, and quarry ponds, to name a few. Find out about possible dive sites in your area by talking to your SSI Dealer, your SSI Instructor, and other divers from your area. You may also want to look into a Specialty Course in *Limited Visibility Diving* or Unique Specialty Courses such as *River Diving* that are designed to fit the local diving needs in your area.

Freshwater Life

Depending on the area of the world where you are diving, you are likely to run into one of a number of fish belonging to a few freshwater families, including Bass, Pike, Perch, Catfish, Trout, Carp, Crappie and Gar (Figure 5-42a & b).

Figure 5-42a   Catfish.

Fresh waters also contain cousins to the more delectable ocean inhabitants, the lobster and clam. Crayfish, commonly known as *crawdad*, are found in almost any type of fresh water. They are much smaller than the lobster, but are edible and considered by some to be very good. Clams can also be found in fresh water, but the only ones recommended for eating are those found in clear, fresh water.

The fresh water food chain is usually formed around floating or rooted plants, but is also abundant around fresh water ship wrecks. There are many famous wrecks in areas such as the Great Lakes of the United States. Fresh water can offer many great dive experiences.

Figure 5-42b   Crappie.

SUMMARY

This chapter is in no way intended to answer all your questions, or address all your concerns regarding dive locations and environments. We have covered some basics here; basics of water and how it behaves, and some basics about what you are likely to see when you go diving. To learn more specifics about water movement you will need to take a SSI Specialty Course in *Waves, Tides and Currents.*

Always work directly with your SSI Dealer and your SSI certified Instructor when planning a dive for a particular location. Find out about water temperatures so that you can determine exposure suit needs. Find out about local water conditions so that you can plan safe dive sites, and safe entries and exits. Don't be timid about inquiring into the quality and reputation of dive expedition businesses and dive boat crews. This is *your* dive, and again, your comfort leads to your enjoyment. Your SSI Dealer is available to answer your questions and help you arrange diving excursions and diving vacations. These Dealers can save you a lot of time and money, while helping prevent travel problems.

Many of the items we did not cover here are more appropriately left for advanced diver courses. Once you get the hang of open water diving, you'll surely become interested in one or several SSI Specialty Courses such as *Wreck Diving, Underwater Photography, Spearfishing,* or *Search and Recovery.*

Lastly, the real sensations of diving can only be experienced in the real setting. Reading this chapter is the blueprint; scuba diving is the completed bridge to a world of discoveries. If you have imagined moving in weightless suspension over the entrancing collage of color and texture we call the coral reef, you will be awestruck the first time you experience it for real.

Your time has come. Let's go diving!

Let's Go Diving!

CHAPTER 6

Chapter 6:
Let's Go Diving!

In case you're wondering—yes, you do know the fundamentals of diving. Now let's put everything together in a comprehensive whole. Since the type of diving you'll be doing may differ greatly from the type of diving other students of the SSI *Open Water Diver* program will be doing, we will not make specific references to geography or particular weather or water conditions, but will cover the minimum information that you'll need to remember no matter what your location and circumstances.

One basic thing you should realize is that there is a significant difference between diving with a group lead by a dive leader and diving on your own (Figure 6-1, next page). As a rule, when diving with a leader, the diving parameters will be outlined for you; when diving on your own without the guidance of a dive leader and/or boat crew, you will have more flexibility in planning dive sites, and dive depths and times, but along with that flexibility will come a greater responsibility. Your SSI *Open Water Diver* course is designed to help you develop the skills needed to deal with these responsibilities. Each class teaches you to become more independent from your Instructor; the independence you will need to become a fully-certified and responsible diver. With Open Water Diver certification comes the duty to stay proficient and to accept responsibility for yourself, whether you are diving with your buddy or with a group.

Figure 6-1   There is a significant difference between diving with a group lead by a dive leader and diving on your own.

This leads us into one of the most important ingredients in enjoyable and responsible diving, the *buddy system.* You may not think of this as essential to knowing *how* to dive, or *what* to do in order to avoid problems while diving, but it is essential to *why* we dive. Diving is a shared experience, and it is only enjoyable to the degree that it *can* be shared. Imagine your excitement upon seeing a gentle giant such as a Manta Ray for the first time, then turning to show it to someone else, but no one is there. Imagine diving a Spanish warship of the 17th century and finding a 300-year-old cannon, then having no one to tell after you surface.

On the surface, buddies provide the kind of necessary assistance that just makes things go so much easier—helping with equipment assembly, and with putting on and taking off equipment (Figure 6-2). You also check the proper positioning and working order of equipment, and your buddy does the same for you. Under water, buddies work together as a team. For example, one buddy can be the leader, in charge of the compass and direction control, while the other buddy monitors depth (Figure 6-3).

Figure 6-2   On the surface, buddies provide the kind of necessary assistance that just makes things go so much easier.

Figure 6-3   Under water, buddies work together as a team.

Another reason for always diving with a buddy is that, naturally, it is safer. In case of a problem, you may need someone there to assist you (Figure 6-4). Conversely, you are needed as a possible helpmate for your buddy. You make a difference to your buddy; you make his or her dive more comfortable just by being there. Having a buddy and being a buddy are closely related to another major objective of any dive; being prepared, and consequently avoiding stress. If you both know what you're doing, if you've planned your dive and you're following the plan, and if you're both ready to deal with something unplanned, you will have assured yourselves of a comfortable dive.

Now let's take a look at one of the most important aspects of diving that we haven't covered in this class yet; learning how to plan the dive.

Figure 6-4   In case of a problem, you may need someone to assist you.

PLANNING THE DIVE

Long before standing at the water's edge with your scuba unit on, you need to discuss the dive with your buddy. There is a natural sequence to this, and it is a good idea to keep a check list as you progress through these steps, being careful to leave nothing out.

The amount of time and energy it takes to plan a dive depends on the environment you will be diving. Some dive trips are practically in your own back yard—just a walk down to the beach, or a quick drive to the local lake. However, some dives will take place in domestic or international locations that require either long car or plane trips. The longer and more complicated the trip is, and the more isolated the location is, the more planning your trip will take. There are three types of planning that take place: Planning for your dive trip; evaluating the destination; and planning at the dive site itself.

PLANNING FOR YOUR DIVE TRIP

Even if you are an experienced traveler, dive travel offers new challenges and adventures. Your first dive trip may come as early as your open water check-out dives, or it may take years to save for. Either way, you'll want your trip to run perfectly. And without help, how do you know what to look for in a dive resort, or how to pick a good charter boat. Plus, all destinations offer different diving and vacation experiences.

■ *Planning Your Trip Thru an SSI Dealer.* Most new divers prefer to take their first few dive trips under the guidance of a professional dive retailer. In fact, many divers enjoy the convenience so much, they continue to take guided trips for years. Your SSI Dealer is there to lead trips, make travel arrangements, and make sure that all of your dives and trip run smoothly. They will help you get yourself and your equipment ready for the trip.

Most new divers take their first few dive trips under the guidance of a professional dive retailer.

■ *Selecting a Resort Operation.* It is important to select a resort or charter operation that caters to entry-level divers (Figure 6-5). When traveling with an SSI Dealer, they will be able to help with such decisions. But if you are traveling on your own, or for your own peace of mind, you may want to confirm the following: cost; number of dives you'll want to do per day, or are allowed per day; number of people per dive/boat; presence of medical facilities; boat features, space, and comfort; and ability level of other divers who will be in the group.

Figure 6-5   It is important to select a resort or charter operation that caters to entry-level divers.

■ *Getting Yourself Ready.* Part of dive planning is getting yourself physically ready for the dive. Physical fitness is important to divers, so if you haven't been exercising lately you may want to hit the weights or the pool for some lap swimming. But remember, before starting a workout routine, you may want to have a physical from a doctor. They can recommend a routine and make sure your heart, lungs and entire body are in shape for diving. If you have a medical contraindication to diving, you may be required to have an updated medical exam before diving. Last, look into taking an SSI *Scuba Skills Update* course if you haven't been diving for a while. An *Update* course is the quickest and easiest way to tune up your diving skills and get ready for your dive.

■ *Getting Your Equipment Ready.*
Check all your equipment ahead of time, too, and have all necessary repairs done. It is best to check your equipment in water—even a swimming pool. If you are going to be using new equipment or a new exposure suit you must understand the functions and features of each item (Figure 6-6). Be sure you have read and understand the owner's manual for each piece of equipment, especially diving computers. If

Figure 6-6   If you are going to be using new equipment or a new exposure suit you must understand the functions and features of each item.

you are planning on renting equipment for your trip, you may want to look into renting it from your SSI Dealer before you go. If it is the same equipment you have been using in class, you may be more comfortable with it; if not, you will still have the chance to test it before jumping into the open water with it.

■ *Taking Along the Proper Paperwork.* It is a good idea to be prepared with the proper paperwork on every trip in order to save time and prevent problems. If you will be completing your open water check-out dives on your dive trip, you will want to be fully prepared.Take along your SSI DiveLog, medical history form and SSI Referral Student Record Card. You obtain these from your local SSI Dealer. Referrals run more smoothly if your local SSI Dealer helps you set it up with the resort you will be traveling to.

If you are traveling as a certified diver you will need your certification credentials (SSI certification card and DiveLog), plus it is a good idea to take a current medical history form. If you are traveling out of the country some of the paper work you may need includes a passport or proof of citizenship, a copy of your travel plans with a local address where you will be staying, and a customs form which registers your camera and electronic equipment with your country of origin.

EVALUATING YOUR DESTINATION

Once you arrive at your dive destination, whether it is the local lake or a remote island, you will need to do some planning and evaluating before diving. This planning can be done when your first arrive, or before you start your dive. How much planning is required is based on how familiar you are with the destination and the type of diving your will be encountering.

■ *Evaluating Local Diving Conditions.* First, decide on where you will be diving and when. Then, become familiar with what sort of weather conditions and water temperatures you'll likely encounter in that place, during that time of day. If you are not diving with an organized group or charter, the local SSI Dealer should be able to provide information about local dive sites (Figure 6-7).

Figure 6-7   If you are not diving with an organized group or charter, the local SSI Dealer should be able to provide information about local dive sites.

These local conditions will affect the type of equipment and exposure suit you will need for the dive, your entry and exit procedures, and particulars such as navigation techniques. Before you leave for your destination, confirm that all the equipment you'll be needing on the dive is present, if not, look into renting or buying it. Finally, get the number(s) for the local emergency medical services and write it in your DiveLog so you are prepared in case of an emergency.

■ *Evaluating Your Physical Condition.* Next, evaluate each other's physical condition. If one of you is sick or very tired, it is not a good idea to go ahead with dive plans hoping that there will be an improvement before or during your dive. On multi-day dive trips, it is easy to get dehydrated, sick, exhausted, or even tired of diving. Be careful to pace yourself, and remember that there is no reason you must dive *every day* (Figure 6-8). Never, for any rea-

Figure 6-8   On multi-day dive trips, it is easy to get dehydrated, sick, exhausted, or even tired of diving. There is no reason you must dive *every day*.

son, feel guilty or embarrassed about aborting dive plans or aborting a dive. This goes not only for health reasons, but also for reasons of apprehension or unpreparedness on the part of one or more divers.

■ *Taking Care of Yourself on Vacation.* Diving at resorts, with charter groups, or in any vacation situation is fun and exciting, but when you elect to dive, make certain you've taken precautions against becoming dehydrated, exhausted, or more susceptible to illness, sinus problems, or decompression sickness. Many things can contribute to these risks.

The sun is a leading contributor to dehydration and related problems. If diving in a hotter climate than you are used to, take precautions to avoid sunburn, heat exhaustion, and heat stroke. Also be aware that your body requires regular rehydration as you perspire. Expose yourself to sunlight moderately, use sun screen, and above all, drink plenty of water.

Another factor you should keep in close check is the typical vacation lifestyle. Drinking alcohol and keeping late hours can lead to dehydration and exhaustion, and contribute to greater risk of decompression sickness (Figure 6-9). When drinking alcohol, know when to quit; unlike many situations, when diving you *really* need to consider your health.

Figure 6-9   Drinking alcohol and keeping late hours can lead to dehydration and exhaustion, and contribute to greater risk of decompression sickness.

Also, never drink alcohol during a dive day. As far as general lifestyle, there is no reason to have to limit your ability to have a good time, but it is ideal to stick to a routine as close as possible to the one you have at home—try to get as much sleep as you normally would, and don't radically change your eating and sleeping schedules. Another bad habit of vacationers is trying to fit in as much recreation as possible in the limited time they have. Some divers will book several dives per day, not accounting for fatigue and extra risk of decompression sickness.

The importance of drinking water is often overlooked, also. Rehydration must be accomplished by drinking water and eating suculent fruits, not by drinking alcohol or soft drinks (Figure 6-10). If you are concerned about the purity of local water, substitute bottled water.

A factor divers often disregard is the temperature of the water they'll be diving in. Even when prepared with correct exposure wear, a diver who does deeper dives into colder water will lose more body

Figure 6-10   Rehydration must be accomplished by drinking water and eating succulent fruits, not by drinking alcohol or soft drinks.

heat, and if repetitive dives are planned, the diver can become very fatigued. Be aware of your physical condition and energy level, and put off a repetitive dive if you are at risk for becoming fatigued.

PLANNING AT THE DIVE SITE

After you make basic plans about your dive trip and destination, it's time to make specific plans about your dive. The amount of time it takes to plan a dive again depends on your familiarity with the site and with your diving buddy. You may spend only a few minutes on the plan itself, or you may want to spend more time discussing your diving preferences, training, hand signals and other critical diving details.

Pre-Dive Briefing

When diving from a charter boat or with any organized group, your diving leader will most likely give a pre-dive briefing about the dive site (Figure 6-11). The briefing may also include specifics such as what your dive parameters are: how long you can stay down, what direction you can swim, how much air to return with in your tank, etc. If the dive is pre-planned such as this, you will not need to put as much time

Figure 6-11   When diving from a charter boat, your diving leader will most likely give a pre-dive briefing about the dive site.

into your plan. When signing up for charters and group dive you may want to find out whether you will be required to follow pre-planned dives and stay with the group. Either way, the following planning information, which is based on the SSI DiveLog page, should be addressed by you and your buddy before diving (Figure 6-12a).

DIVE NUMBER _____

SSI® Scuba Schools International **DiveLog**

Date _____ Buddy _____

Site Name _____

Location _____

Directions _____

Dive Objective _____

CONDITIONS

Water: ☐ Salt ☐ Fresh Temperature _____ Visibility _____
Surface: ☐ Calm ☐ Choppy ☐ Rough
Surf: ☐ Small ☐ Medium ☐ Large **Tide:** ☐ High ☐ Low
Current: ☐ Fast ☐ Slow Type _____
Weather: ☐ Sunny ☐ Cloudy Temperature _____
Thermocline: Temperature _____ Depth _____

EQUIPMENT

Suit: ☐ Dive Skin ☐ Polartec ☐ 6mm ☐ 3mm ☐ Drysuit
Tank Size: _____ ☐ Steel ☐ Aluminum AIR ON?
Tank Pressure: Start _____ End _____ SCR _____
Other Equipment: ☐ Compass ☐ Dive Light ☐ Knife ☐ Camera
☐ Game Bag ☐ *Next Time Take* _____
Weight: Amount _____ ☐ OK* ☐ Next TimeTry _____

* If weight is ok, record it permanently on the Proper Weighting Tables in the Equipment Record section of this DiveLog.

BUDDY CHECK

☐ Hand Signals
☐ Lost Buddy
☐ Air Sharing Ascent
☐ Emergency Ascent
☐ _____

☐ Power Inflator Location & Use
☐ Alternate Air Source Location & Use
☐ Weight System Location & Use
☐ _____
☐ _____

DIVE PLAN

| Repetitive Group | ABT _____ + _____ = TBT: | Repetitive Group | Surface Interval | Repetitive Group (For next dive today) |

_____   15 FT.
Depth   Bottom Time (TBT)   3 MIN.

	PLANNED	CONTINGENCY
MAX DEPTH		
MAX TIME		

Time: In _____ **Out** _____
Hours this dive: _____ **Total:** _____
First time at this site? ☐ Yes ☐ No

Witness Signature: _____

© 1977 Concept Systems, Inc. • Revised 1986, '89, '90, '92, '95   SQ-6 • DIVELOG'95 fldr • "Log Page LVL1-5 '95" • 7/95 • Art File #1100-G

Figure 6-12a The SSI DiveLog page.

■ **Objective of the Dive.** When making your own dive plan first, talk about why you're diving, and make sure you are both in agreement about your objective. Are you going just to explore coral reefs? Do you plan to investigate a wreck site? Communicate about these things beforehand, and don't suddenly "spring" a new idea on your buddy after your dive has begun; that would not be fair to a buddy who may feel apprehensive about doing something that only *you* find challenging. Pressuring an unprepared diver is a sure way of causing stress that can lead to an accident (see Figure 6-12a, page 195).

■ **Conditions of the Dive.** Your SSI DiveLog provides a convenient check list for site conditions. The type of water, weather, and water movement, such as surf and current, may effect different aspects of your dive, such as entries and exits, the amount of thermal protection to wear, how much air you consume, and your direction and ability to navigate (see Figure 6-12a, page 195).

■ **Equipment.** Go over the convenient Equipment Check list in your SSI DiveLog when planning your dive. Knowing what type of suit you wore, tank size, special equipment and amount of weight may come in handy when planning future dives, plus it provides a pre-dive checklist to make sure your equipment is ready for diving. When boat diving, plan your dive and your equipment assembly, donning, and adjustment such that you are ready to enter the water when the boat reaches the dive site. On chartered trips most decisions may be made for you, but it is certainly smart to check with the captain or dive leader to determine when to get dressed and don equipment.

If you are unfamiliar with your buddy, or if you and your buddy haven't been diving in a while, you may want to discuss the following *Buddy Check Procedures* (see Figure 6-12a, page 195). These procedures cover some of the differences you may have in your diving skills, emergency training, and type of equipment.

■ **Communication.** Coordinate the hand signals you'll use with your buddy, and discuss any other forms of communication you might use during the dive, or on the surface, in an emergency.

■ **Lost Buddy Procedure.** Discuss a lost or separated buddy procedure. Discuss how long you will look for your buddy should you become separated and when you will surface for help. One recommended procedure is to make two or three 360° turns in the water, looking for bubbles or other signs of your buddy. If other divers are near, you can signal them to find out if they have seen your buddy. If he is no where to be found it is best to surface normally and if your buddy has not surfaced, get help immediately. One reason to dive with a charter or group is the fact that there are other support personnel to assist in an emergency.

■ **Emergency Skills Training.** Discuss how each of you was trained in emergency skills such as air sharing ascents and emergency ascents, because the time to find out is not under water in an emergency. If you discuss your training ahead of time you can be better prepared to handle an emergency.

■ **Equipment Familiarization.** Familiarize yourselves with each other's equipment. What type of power inflator does your buddy have and how does it work? Where is your buddy's alternate air source located and how does it work? What type of configuration is his or her weight system, and how does it detach?

■ **Entry and Exit Procedures.** If you're diving from a boat, you will be informed of the entry and exit procedures, However, if you are diving by yourselves, you and your buddy should discuss the safest and easiest methods. Ask your local SSI Dealer if you are unfamiliar with the procedures for the local diving conditions.

■ **No-Decompression Dive Plan and Dive Parameters.** Your next step is to plan a no-decompression dive using the Doppler limits on the U.S. Navy Dive Tables. Plan your maximum depth and time and have a contingency plan. Plus, you may want to pre-plan your surface interval and what you'll do during that time. You should also discuss your minimum tank pressure before resurfacing (it is recommended that you be on the surface with no less than 500 psi or 35 bar). Again, some of these decisions may be made for you when diving with a charter or group. The dive profile in your SSI DiveLog will help you record your parameters and plan a repetitive dive (Figure 6-12b).

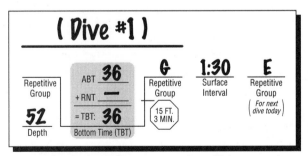

Figure 6-12b   The dive profile in your SSI DiveLog will help you record your parameters and plan a repetitive dive.

■ **Go/No-Go Diving Decision.** Last, confirm that both you and your buddy are feeling okay and are still ready to make the dive. Each diver has the right at any time, for any reason, to call off a dive, even if you are dressed and ready to enter the water.

SUMMARY OF DIVING PROCEDURES

Although we will not review the entire diving procedure again, we have created this handy summary which reviews each phase of the dive and has been reduced to twenty main procedures. The SSI *Open Water Diver* video part six, *Let's Go Diving!*, is a great visual summary for these twenty diving procedures.

1. Plan the dive.

2. Assemble and adjust your diving equipment.

3. Complete a final pre-entry buddy check before entry.

4. Confirm your direction, including how you handle any current.

5. Make the safest and easiest entry for the conditions.

6. Follow proper descent procedures, using a line if possible, and equalizie ear pressure.

7. Stay with your buddy or the group throughout the dive.

8. Use natural and/or compass navigation to avoid getting lost under water.

9. Monitor your instruments and stick to the dive plan.

10. Breathe normally all the time, stay relaxed and have fun!

11. Maintain neutral buoyancy throughout the dive to conserve energy and avoid damaging the environment.

12. Ascend at the same rate as your buddy, and no faster than 30 feet per minute (9 metres per minute).

13. Make a safety stop at 15 feet (5 metres) for 3 to 5 minutes.

14. Follow proper surface procedures by inflating your BC and keeping your mask and regulator in place.

15. Make the safest and easiest exit for the diving conditions. Stay clear of the boat's dive platform or ladder until it is your turn to exit.

16. Help each other gear down from the dive.

17. Get plenty of rest and fluids during your surface interval.

18. Plan and prepare for the next dive if you are making one.

19. Clean and store your equipment according to the manufacturer's recommendations.

20. Log each dive in your SSI DiveLog as you work toward upgrading your certification to a more advanced status!

WHERE DO YOU GO FROM HERE?

As you near completion of your *Open Water Diver* course, SSI congratulates you. Not for successful completion of the course, because you'll still need to fulfill your water requirements for that. What we congratulate you on is being the kind of person to accept a challenge, one which teaches you new skills, requires the mastering of equipment and safety techniques, and allows you to enter into an adventure and write a new episode in the story of your life. As a scuba diver you accept the responsibilities that accompany certification, but you also gain the freedom to enjoy this wonderful new underwater world! (Figure 6-13)

Figure 6-13   As a scuba diver you accept the responsibilities that accompany certification, but you also gain the freedom to enjoy this wonderful new world!

ACTIVITIES FOR THE CERTIFIED DIVER

So what types of adventures are available to the certified diver? There are more than you can imagine, and we will only mention a few of them here. You can find out more specifics about these underwater activities from your local SSI Dealer, or from anywhere you travel to. While some diving activities can be done anywhere, others are specific to a geographic region or diving environment. This is part of the fun of dive travel—seeking out new activities and adventures wherever you happen to go. And your travel need not be exotic, for diving adventures can be found in some of the most peculiar and unpredictable places.

■ *Boat Diving.* Explore remote dive sites only accessible by boat.

■ *Night/Limited Visibility Diving.* Explore the underwater world at night through the use of lights, or respect and enjoy an environment with little or no visibility (Figure 6-14).

■ *Deep Diving.* Scuba diving beyond the recreational depth limits requires additional planning and skills.

Figure 6-14   Explore the underwater world at night through the use of lights.

■ *Navigation.* Compass and natural navigation techniques allow you to control your direction and gain confidence under water (Figure 6-15).

■ *Wreck Diving and Archaeology.* Learn to explore and respect underwater shipwrecks, and if you want to learn more, archaeology teaches you how to research and preserve these precious resources (Figure 6-16).

Figure 6-15   Compass and natural navigation techniques allow you to control your direction.

■ *Search and Recovery.* Whether recovering a treasure or the anchor from your boat, learn the techniques needed to search and recover items under water.

Figure 6-16   Learn to explore and respect underwater shipwrecks.

▲ Figure 6-17a

Capture your diving memories on
film or video after you learn about
photography and videography.

Figure 6-17b ▶

■ *Photography and Videography.* Capture your diving memories on film or video after you learn about photography and videography. These are two of diving's most popular activities (Figure 6-17 a & b).

■ *Hunting and Game Collecting.* Learn to hunt and collect game such as fish and lobsters. However, this activity is under government control and may not be legal in all parts of the world, or at all times of the year.

■ *Marine Identification.* Learn to identify the fish and marine animals you see under water. Courses are offered in different regions so you can learn about marine life in different diving environments.

■ *Reef Ecology.* We all know how precious our underwater reefs are so we should really learn to protect them. Many Dealers and Resorts offer courses in advanced buoyancy control and reef ecology (Figure 6-18).

Figure 6-18 Many Dealers and Resorts offer courses in advanced buoyancy control and reef ecology.

■ ***Computer Diving.*** Computers are sophisticated pieces of equipment and require additional training in their use. You will learn how to track your vital diving information and maximize bottom time .

While some diving activities involve special equipment or skills, others, such as those listed below, revolve around geography and the diving environment.

■ ***Cavern Diving.*** Many parts of the world have caverns that are available to divers. By learning the physical and mental skills needed for cavern diving you will increase your comfort and ability.

■ ***Dry Suit and Cold Water Diving.*** Most cold water diving environments require specialized skills and equipment such as dry suits. Learn how to enjoy the cold water and the adventure it provides (Figure 6-19).

■ ***Kelp Diving.*** If you are familiar with reefs, get ready for a new adventure. Kelp diving offers a unique activity that is unmatched. A background in kelp diving techniques will enhance your diving experience (see Figure 6-19).

Figure 6-19 Most cold water diving environments require specialized skills and equipment such as dry suits.

■ ***Waves and Drift Diving.*** As you learned in Chapter 5, the aquatic environment and the movement of its waters can be a powerful force. However, by learning more about waves, tides and currents you can enjoy new activities such as drift diving and shore diving.

■ ***River Diving.*** Rivers offer a new adventure once you learn to deal with the mechanics of how the water in the river flows.

■ ***High Altitude Diving.*** The high altitude lakes and rivers in our mountains offer a new variety of underwater life and adventure, but they pose decompression risks. Some special training will open up this new activity.

■ ***Oil Rig Diving.*** The giant oil rigs in our oceans house an abundance of marine life by creating artificial reef structures. Once some training is received, these rigs open up a new world to divers.

While there are more diving activities available than we can mention, this should give you a taste of the numerous adventures available to the certified diver. You must understand, however, that just because you are a certified diver does not mean you are qualified to perform every type of diving. In fact, you are only trained in the conditions you have actually dived in—shore diving, boat diving, or reef diving. Your experience is currently limited to your open water training dives.

So how do you get involved in these activities? The quickest and easiest way to get involved in new diving activities is through continuing education. SSI's Specialty Diver Courses are your shortcut to learning, your expressway to knowledge! (Figure 6-20)

In fact, you should think of your *Open Water Diver* training as the "basic model." Specialties, then, would be the "options" that "customize" your training to your exact needs. Take whatever courses that build the skills for your type of diving. For example, your dream may be to photograph reef fish, and you think you'll dive mostly from boats. Some good specialties for you to consider would be *Boat Diving, Marine Identification, Underwater Photography* and possibly *Navigation* or *Reef Ecology.* Combinations of Specialty Courses create "build your own" advanced ratings from SSI.

Figure 6-20 The quickest and easiest way to get involved in new diving activities is through continuing education.

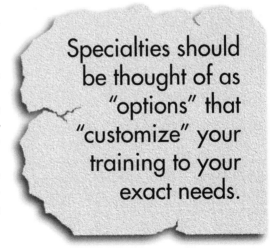

Specialties should be thought of as "options" that "customize" your training to your exact needs.

BECOMING A SPECIALTY DIVER

SSI's Specialty Diver Program is flexible and designed to meet the needs of the individual diver. You choose the courses that fit your interests. Each SSI Dealer will offer a variety of Specialty Courses, including some that are specific to the diving environment in your area. If you live near the ocean, you can find out more about waves, tides and currents. Inland divers may be interested in river or high altitude diving. You can also take courses while you are traveling as a way to broaden your knowledge level.

Once you are certified in two sepa-rate Specialty Courses, such as Boat Diving and Deep Diving, you are eli-gible to become a *Specialty Diver* (Figure 6-21). The only other require-ment is to log 12 dives. You will have logged 5 dives in open water training and another 4 during specialty train-ing; this means you must complete 3 more experience dives on your own. This should not be a problem for an enthusiastic diver such as yourself.

Figure 6-21   Once you are certified in two sep-arate Specialty Courses, you are eligible to become a Specialty Diver.

BECOMING AN ADVANCED OPEN WATER DIVER

The goal of many new divers is to complete an Advanced course. When you receive an *Advanced Open Water Diver* card from SSI, you know that you are truly an advanced diver (Figure 6-22). We care enough to make our course flexible, yet chal-lenging—resulting in a card you'll be proud to carry.

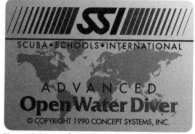

Figure 6-22   When you receive an Advanced Open Water Diver card from SSI, you know that you are truly an advanced diver.

To become an Advanced Open Water Diver you must complete four Specialty Courses. You select the four courses you want, taking them at your own leisure. This may take one week, or one year—it's up to you. You can also take an *Advanced Open Water Diver* course from your SSI Authorized Dealer. Your Dealer will package four courses such as Boat Diving, Navigation, Wreck Diving and Deep Diving, that fit the local diving needs and offer them as a complete course. Again, once you have completed the training you must complete the experience requirement, which is done by logging a total of 24 dives. This requirement of training plus experience is what sets the SSI advanced rating apart, plus it is the key to creating an advanced diver.

You can't learn to dive from a book—you need to get out there and spend some time in the water!

BECOMING A MASTER DIVER

The *Master Diver* rating is SSI's most prestigious diver rating (Figure 6-23). When you carry this card, you carry the pride and experience that accompanies it. To become an SSI *Master Diver* is no easy task for it takes diving experience. Once you earn your Advanced Open Water Diver rating you have one more training requirement—the SSI **Diver Stress and Rescue** Course. This is

Figure 6-23 The Master Diver rating is SSI's most prestigious diver rating.

the Specialty Course that helps divers learn to help themselves and others when diving. It creates a new level of confidence and ability in the diver that cannot be earned through any other course.

To complete the experience requirement the diver must log a total of 50 dives. This is quite an accomplishment, and once you reach the 50 dive mark you will understand why this number was chosen. It takes the average diver 50 or more dives to achieve the kind of ability needed to feel truly comfortable in the water. At this point divers are ready to call themselves *Master Divers!*

BECOMING A DIVING LEADER

Scuba diving is the kind of sport that can become addictive to many individuals. Once they take that first plunge into the beautiful blue ocean they're hooked! So what kind of opportunities are available to a diving enthusiast? Your future as a diving leader can include many options— from working at a dive resort to helping out at the local retail store (Figure 6-24). If you are interested in getting into diving leadership, our best advice

Figure 6-24 Your future as a diving leader can include many options—from working at a dive resort to helping out at the local retail store.

is to get plenty of training and diving experience. SSI offers leadership training courses for the *Dive Control Specialist* and all levels of instructor from *Open Water Instructor* to *Instructor Certifier*. Contact your local SSI Authorized Dealer or ask your SSI Instructor about the many travel, business and career options that exist for diving leaders.

THE SSI DIVELOG SYSTEM

By now you have come to realize how important logging dives is to the SSI system; thus we have created a series of DiveLogs that truly fit the needs of an active, dedicated diver. For we care enough to provide the SSI diver with the very best products we can produce, and the SSI DiveLog system is one of our most innovative concepts. We were the first scuba certification agency to incorporate such a DiveLog into our training system; a DiveLog that offers the diver recognition for both training and diving, and we are proud of it.

THE TOTAL DIVELOG

The SSI *Total DiveLog* is the foundation for the entire SSI teaching system. As you can see by the DiveLog flow chart (see Figure 6-25), SSI offers two paths for the diver: the training path and the experience path. The training path has already been explained. You have the option of earning various levels of certification cards such as the *Specialty Diver* card, the *Advanced Open Water Diver* card and the *Master Diver* card. However, the SSI Total DiveLog allows you to earn recognition whether you take any additional training or not. We achieve this through a series of milestones we have named Levels 1 thru 5, which you achieve by logging dives. When you complete one of these levels you receive a sticker on your Open Water Diver card that indicates how many dives you have logged. This sticker shows to dive resorts and charter boats that you are more experienced than the average *Open Water Diver* because you have logged a number of dives. This comes in handy when dive operators will only allow you to make certain dives if you have a certain level of experience. It will keep you from diving from the "beginner" boat for the rest of your life. When you have logged a monumental 100 dives you become eligible to receive the prestigious *Century Diver* card.

There are many practical reasons for logging dives. For one, it helps maintain an accurate dive profile which allows you to plan safe, repetitive dives. In addition, you can record valuable information about the dives you make, such as the dive location, directions, weather and water conditions. Keeping a history of your air consumption rates will track your comfort level because lower rates indicate greater comfort. It is also a good idea to keep track of the amount of weight you use to achieve neutral buoyancy. By keeping track of weight needs in different circumstances, you'll be able to know in advance how much weight you'll require for a particular dive. You may also want to make notations on what kinds of equipment you used, and what you should purchase before your next dive.

You are probably beginning to see that a DiveLog is a handy tool with many purposes. In addition to tracking your number of logged dives, your SSI DiveLog is an important source of information for subsequent dives, for keeping track of your training, and for recording memories (Figure 6-26). The DiveLog is also a record-keeping system for the SSI Specialty Diver and *Scuba Skills Update* programs. The Equipment section helps you record purchases, maintenance, your weighting needs for proper buoyancy, and serves as a pre-trip checklist.

The DiveLog is a valuable tool. Each diver must use a DiveLog during Open Water Diver training. Your DiveLog may only provide Levels 1 and 2, which is all you need for your initial training. Your SSI Dealer offers refills for Levels 3, 4 and 5 that you can add to your DiveLog. You may also want to upgrade your binder to the deluxe *Total DiveLog* binder with a velcro closure. Why not? A serious diver deserves only the best DiveLog.

Figure 6-25   The Total DiveLog flowchart.

Figure 6-26   Your SSI DiveLog is an important source of information for subsequent dives, for keeping track of your training, and for recording memories.

THE PLATINUM DIVELOG

When a diver completes all five levels of the Total DiveLog, or has logged 100 dives, it is time to move up to SSI's *Platinum DiveLog* (Figure 6-27). This DiveLog holds enough pages to log 400 more dives, which should be enough for all but the most prolific diver! As you can see by the accompanying flowchart, the Platinum DiveLog is again designed to offer recognition at each diving milestone (Figure 6-28). When you complete Level 6 you have completed 200 logged dives; at Level 7 you will have completed 300 logged dives; at Level 8, 400 logged dives; and at Level 9 you will have logged over 500 logged dives. While you receive a sticker to commemorate each 100 logged dive milestone, you also become eligible to receive the *Gold 500 Diver* card when you reach 500 dives. At Level 10, when you complete an incredible 1000 logged dives, you become eligible to receive the prestigious *Platinum 1000 Diver* card. To receive your recognition stickers, or to receive your *Gold 500* or *Platinum 1000 Diver* card, simply go to your SSI Dealer to have your logged dives verified. He can apply your stickers right there, and order your cards from SSI Headquarters. As you can imagine, only the most dedicated divers with years of diving experience could ever hope to earn these two prestigious recognition levels. But isn't that what makes them all the more worthwhile!

Figure 6-27   When a diver has logged 100 dives, it is time to move up to SSI's *Platinum DiveLog.*

And for divers who have dedicated their life to the sport of diving, those who have logged an unbelievable 5000 dives, SSI offers the Platinum Pro 5000 Diver card. This card can only be award- ed, not purchased, for it is only avail- able to the truly elite of diving. *Skin Diver* magazine termed it the "most desirable card in diving," and that is what is has become since it was first awarded in 1993. Most of div- ing's most well- known and elite fig- ures carry an SSI Platinum Pro 5000 Diver card (Figure 6- 29). Perhaps your Instructor has one.

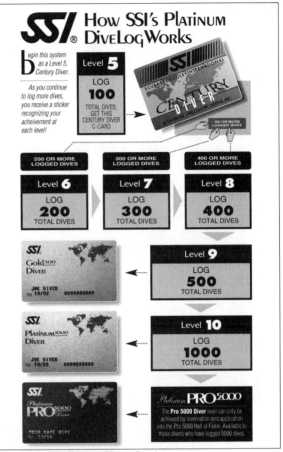

Figure 6-28   The Platinum DiveLog flowchart.

Figure 6-29   Most of diving's most well-known and elite figures carry an SSI Platinum Pro 5000 Diver card.

SUMMARY

Look back now and notice what you've accomplished. Just a short time ago you knew very little, if anything, about scuba diving. You have also learned in this short time some things you've never known about your body, and about a part of our world which is often seen from above, but seldom seen or understood below the surface.

Now it is your choice what to do with this new knowledge. You are, however, invited to make it your passion, just as many thousands of others have the world over. The diving experience is travel, adventure, new friends, and exotic scenery. You are not just learning a new sport, but entering into a new lifestyle—one which can easily be addicting. Scuba diving has a mystique about it, unlike any other sport. You'll begin to see why once you embark on the fantastic journey that awaits you in the underwater world.

As a final word, this sport, more so than others, requires being in contact with your local Dealer and Instructor. You will want to acquire your own equipment so that it becomes very familiar to you (Figure 6-30). It is important to personalize. You will get used to the configurations of your own BC and automatically know where the inflator hose is located, exactly how the power inflator is operated, and where to locate your dump valve quickly. Your wet suit will fit so well that you will hardly notice it—you'll simply be comfortable in the water. In short, your personal equipment will become an extension of your body.

Figure 6-30 You will want to acquire your own equipment so that it becomes very familiar to you.

Work with the experts at your local SSI Dealer to determine your needs, then acquire the equipment that will gradually become your best friend—next to your dive buddy. Also see your dive store and instructor about the next step—Specialty and Advanced Diver courses in your particular areas of interest. Once you get hooked, there's no limit to what you can go on to do in your future as a diver.

Whatever your needs and aspirations, your answers lie somewhere in the network of SSI Authorized Dealers, SSI Instructors, and at SSI Headquarters. We've helped you start diving and we'd like to see you keep diving—because we care about you and your needs as a diver!

Glossary

OF
DIVING
TERMS

actual bottom time (ABT)

compressed air

decompression dive

group designation letter

independent air source

proper weighting

submersible pressure gauge (SPG)

wet suit

Glossary
OF DIVING TERMS

actual bottom time (ABT) The actual amount of time a diver spent under water on a repetitive scuba dive.

air embolism When a diver fails to exhale on ascent, overexpansion of the lungs can create a condition in which air bubbles are forced into the circulatory system which may form a blockage of the flow of blood to body tissues such as the brain.

air sharing An out-of-air situation in which a donor provides a needer an air source either by passing the primary or secondary regulator and then breathing off the other, or by passing the donor's primary regulator back and forth between donor and needer, or by providing the needer with an independent air system.

air sharing ascent An out-of-air ascent after air sharing has been established, and which can be aided by one or both buoyancy compen-sators.

alternate air source A second air source carried by the diver to be used for air sharing, or in the event the primary air source fails; may come in the form of an octopus regulator, an independent system such as a pony bottle, or as part of the power inflator system.

altitude dive Any dive more than 1000 feet (300 metres) above sea level. The U.S. Navy Dive Tables are not accurate above 1000 feet; special altitude tables must be used.

ambient pressure The total pressure surrounding the diver at a given depth. The sum of the air pressure and water pressure.

atmosphere By convention, the pressure exerted at sea level by a column of air 64 miles (103 km) high and 1 inch (25 mm) square (abbreviated as ATM).

atmospheric pressure The pressure exerted by 1 ATM of air at sea level, expressed as 14.7 pounds per square inch (1 bar).

bends, the A colloquial term for decompression sickness which is de-rived from the bent position a victim may take due to pain in the joints.

bottom time The amount of elapsed time from the start of your descent, to the time you begin your direct ascent back to the surface.

buoyancy compensator (BC) A device worn by a diver used to regulate buoyancy under water or as a surface flotation device. It should be equipped with an oral inflator, power inflator, and dump valve mechanism.

buoyant ascent An ascent aided by inflation of the buoyancy compensator.

certification card An identification card that is achieved by completing a diver certification course, and which is required in order to rent diving equipment or purchase compressed air, and participate in trips and activities available only to certified divers.

compass An instrument used for determining direction under water using the earth's magnetic field.

compressed air Air that is purified and condensed to greater than atmospheric pressure through the use of an air compressor.

corals Colonial animals that lay down a skeleton of limestone and harbor a colorful microscopic plant life.

crustaceans Arthropods, which are usually aquatic, with a segmented body and paired, jointed limbs—lobsters and crabs, for example.

decompression dive A dive that exceeds the no-decompression time limits of the U.S. Navy Dive Tables, thus requiring planned decompression stops to eliminate excess nitrogen accumulated during the dive.

decompression illness A term which describes both overexpansion injuries, including arterial gas embolism (AGE), and decompression sickness (DCS) for purposes of treatment.

decompression sickness A condition resulting from inadequate release of excess nitrogen absorbed during a dive.

depth The deepest point reached during the dive, no matter how briefly you stayed there.

depth gauge A pressure-sensitive instrument used to determine depth under water; may include a maximum depth indicator.

dive computer An instrument which electronically calculates a diver's no-decompression limits and decompression requirements on a single dive or series of dives, in addition to providing other information such as depth, bottom time, surface interval time, and proper ascent rate.

dive tables Tables created by the U.S. Navy which provide information to the diver on nitrogen absorption based on depth and bottom time. Allows the diver to plan no-decompression dives, and repetitive dives.

Doppler limits More conservative recommended no-decompression time limits at depth than the U.S. Navy time limits, based on Doppler Ultrasound Research.

dry suit An exposure suit used in colder waters which prevents water entry through seals at the neck and wrists.

emergency swimming ascent A swimming ascent to the surface under stressful or emergency conditions, where the diver releases the weight system upon reaching the surface to achieve maximum positive buoyancy.

emergency buoyant ascent A swimming ascent performed in an out-of-air situation where the diver releases the weight system at depth to achieve immediate positive buoyancy.

equalization The process of injecting a greater amount of gas into an air space so that the pressure inside the space is the same as pressure outside or surrounding the space.

exposure suit A diving suit that is worn to protect the diver from exposure to the elements (sun, abrasion, cold). Also known as dry suit, wet suit, lycra dive suit.

fins Footwear worn by a scuba diver or snorkeler to substantially increase the power and efficiency of the kicking motion. Fins reduce the amount of energy needed to swim a certain distance.

first-stage The part of the regulator system that is attached to the tank valve, and reduces the pressure of the compressed air from the tank to approximately 100-150 psi (7-10 bar) over ambient pressure.

group designation letter The letter assigned after a dive which indicates the amount of residual nitrogen remaining in the diver's tissues.

hyperventilation Rapid, shallow, sometimes uncontrolled breathing which is often stress or fear induced, and results in carbon dioxide buildup causing light-headedness and an out-of-air feeling.

hypothermia A condition that occurs when the body's core tem-perature drops below the normal temperature of 98.6°F (37°C). Symptoms include confusion, bluing of the skin, rigidity, and loss of coordination.

hypoxia Deficiency in the amount of oxygen reaching bodily tissues; oxygen starvation.

hyperbaric chamber A chamber which can be pressurized and is used to treat air embolism, decompression sickness, and other over-expansion problems.

independent air source A small, additional air bottle that is carried by the diver for use in an out-of-air situation. Also known as alternate air source, pony bottle.

inflator-integrated air source An extra second stage built into the buoyancy compensator inflator hose, or integrated into the power inflator mechanism. Also known as alternate air source.

instrument console A console that usually consists of the depth and pressure gauge, and may include a compass, timing device and diving computer; attached to the first stage of the regulator via the pressure gauge.

invertebrate An animal which lacks a backbone or spinal column.

mask Diving equipment worn over the eyes and nose to provide an air pocket for better vision and equalization of pressure.

negative buoyancy The tendency or capacity for a diver to sink when immersed in water.

neutral buoyancy The tendency or capacity for a diver to neither sink nor float when immersed in water.

no-decompression dive Any dive that can be made to a certain depth for a maximum amount of time so that a direct ascent can be made to the surface; a dive that does not require decompression stops in order to reduce excess nitrogen.

no-decompression limits Maximum specified times at given depths from which decompression stops are not required upon return to the surface as designated on the dive tables.

octopus regulator An additional second-stage. Also known as alternate air source.

oral inflator An inflation device on the buoyancy compensator which allows the BC to be inflated by placing it in the diver's mouth and using air from the lungs.

overexpansion injuries Injury caused by air escaping from the lungs during ascent because of failure to exhale on ascent after breathing compressed air. Also known as air embolism, mediastinal emphysema, pneumothorax, subcutaneous emphysema.

pelagic Living in open seas rather than waters adjacent to land or inland waters.

positive buoyancy The tendency or capacity for a diver to float when immersed in water.

power inflator A device on a buoyancy compensator which is attached to the low pressure port on the first stage of the regulator, and allows quick inflation by using air from the tank.

proper weighting The amount of weight required to keep a diver neutrally buoyant throughout a dive. This includes being able to descend below the surface at the beginning of the dive, remain neutral during the dive, and stay neutral at the end of the dive when the tank may become more buoyant due to low tank pressure.

regulator An apparatus which is attached to the air supply (tank) and is activated by inhalation; consists of a first-stage and second-stage. Also known as demand regulator.

repetitive dive Any dive started within 10 minutes to 12 hours after a previous scuba dive.

residual nitrogen time (RNT) Excessive nitrogen pressure still residual in the diver at the beginning of a repetitive dive, expressed in minutes of exposure at the planned repetitive dive depth.

safety stop An added safety measure of 3 to 5 minutes at 10 to 30 feet that divers should take after no-decompression dives to help reduce "silent bubbles" and the risk of pressure related injuries.

scuba The acronym for "self-contained underwater breathing apparatus." The word used to describe the equipment which consists of a demand regulator and a compressed air tank that is carried on the diver's back.

second-stage The part of the regulator that fits in the diver's mouth, reduces the air pressure from 100-150 psi over ambient pressure, and supplies the air to the diver at breathing pressure on demand. Also known as regulator mouthpiece.

snorkel An open tube which extends from the mouth to the surface, and allows the snorkeler or scuba diver to breathe comfortably on the surface with the face in the water.

snorkeling Diving with the aid of mask, fins, snorkel, and BC and without the aid of scuba diving equipment. Also known as breath-hold diving, free diving, skin diving.

squeeze A condition of discomfort caused by a difference in pressure on an enclosed air space within the body or equipment: Ear, sinus, mask, suit.

submersible pressure gauge (SPG) An instrument that is attached to the high-pressure port on the first-stage of the regulator and allows the diver to monitor how much air pressure remains in the scuba tank. Also known as pressure gauge.

surface interval The amount of time the diver stays out of the water or on the surface between dives, beginning as soon as the diver surfaces and ending at the start of the next descent.

tank A hollow metal (aluminum or steel) high-pressure cylinder which is sealed with a retaining valve, and is used to carry compressed air under water.

total bottom time (TBT) The time divers must use to calculate their new repetitive group designation at the end of a repetitive dive. Calculated as *actual bottom time (ABT) + residual nitrogen time (RNT) = total bottom time (TBT).*

turbid Having sediment or foreign particles stirred up or suspended; muddy, cloudy, limited visibility.

weight belt A device worn around the diver's waist and attached with a quick-release buckle, which allows the diver to offset the positive buoyancy caused by exposure suits.

wet suit An exposure suit, commonly made of foam neoprene, which provides thermal insulation.